CB

Kenya

Front cover: Maasai Mara
National Reserve
Right: A Kenyan Rock Agama

TOP 10 ATTRACTIONS

Maasai Mara Named after the Maasai people, the reserve is famed for its lions and annual wildebeest migration (page 72)

The Amboseli With its impressive Mount Kilimanjaro backdrop, few places are as spectacular for elephant spotting (page 76)

Rift Valley Lakes Nakuru and Bogoria host millions flamingos, but all the lakes support a rich birdlife (pag

Kenya's coast Character gorgeous white san palm trees (pag

savo East and West The largest national park in Kenya, and one of the wildest in character (page 76)

Mount Kenya Part of the Central Highlands, this extinct volcano offers spectacular views (page 54)

airobi The country's ustling capital is the first stop or most visitors (page 45)

Mombasa This historic Swahili trade port, with medieval trade links to Arabia and Asia, is Kenya's oldest city (page 80)

mu Visiting this ancient and town is like stepping ck in time (page 89)

Samburu National Reserve See beautiful landscapes and species found only in the north of the country (page 57)

A PERFECT TOUR

Day 1-2 Nairobi

The modern capital is the perfect climatic introduction to Kenya. A full day here can be divided between the informative National Museum, the evocative Karen Blixen Museum, and a game drive through Nairobi National Park, where lions, rhinos and other wildlife roam below the city skyscrapers.

Day 4-5 Samburu-Buffalo Springs

Descend by road to these twin reserves at the edge of the northern deserts, where game viewing – including Grevy's zebra and the reticulated giraffe – focuses on the muddy Ewaso Nyiro River, and a fringing strand of lush riparian woodland.

Day 3 Tree Hotels of the Central Highlands

A two to three hour drive north of Nairobi leads to the central highlands below Mt Kenya, where a trio of 'tree hotels' overlooking waterholes offer superb in-house game viewing. Serena Mountain Lodge (see page 55) is the pick for forest wildlife, but Treetops (see page 52), with its royalist associations, has the sentimental edge.

Day 6 Lake Nakuru

Following an early start and a mid-morning stop at the spectacular Thomson's Falls outside Nyahururu, head down to Lake Nakuru National Park, a compact main park famed for its flamingos, and white and black rhino.

OF KENYA

Day 10-11 Lake Naivasha

This pretty freshwater lake is the gateway for several boating and walking excursions, from the challenging ascent of volcanic Mt Longonot, to a relaxed stroll on tiny Crescent Island.

Day 12-13 Amboseli

It's a long drive from Naivasha to Amboseli, but the effort is justified by the rewards: stirring dusk views of snow-capped Kilimanjaro, and perhaps the best elephant viewing in Africa.

Day 16-21 Coastal break

Dedicate your last five nights to Kenya's wonderful Indian Ocean coastline, with its beautiful beaches and mysterious medieval ruins, and wonderful diving and snorkelling. Diani Beach, south of Mombasa, is favoured by sun-worshippers, while Watamu will thrill more restless travellers with its wide range of marine and terrestrial activities.

Day 7-9 Maasai Mara

The game-viewing pinnacle of any Kenyan safari, about four hours' drive from Nakuru, the magical Maasai Mara is home to some of Africa's largest concentrations of big cats and antelope.

Day 14-15 Tsavo East and West

Take a relaxed drive to the coast over two days through Tsavo, stopping for a night at each of its western and eastern components. Tsavo West's lush Mzima Springs provide a bizarre contrast to the scenic austerity of the immense Tsavo East.

CONTENTS

26

32

97

103

Features

11

92

INTRODUCTION

Travel through Kenya and you will see all of Africa in one country. If you drive cross-country, you will be surprised how quickly the landscape changes: dropping down from fertile highlands into semi-arid plains, emerging from a lush mountain forest to sweep through a vast plateau, climbing up a steep escarpment from the immense chasm that is the Rift Valley, or turning off coconut palm-lined tarmac on to a dusty dirt track.

Kenya is a country of contradictions, where snow lies on the equator, and semi-deserts flood in the long rains. Blue lakes turn pink when blanketed with a million flamingos; the icy top of Mount Kilimanjaro shimmers over Amboseli's arid plains. In contrast to the rich diversity of the southwest – home to 85 percent of the population – the vast northern and eastern regions, nearly two-thirds of the country, are wilderness.

The country has long been a favourite safari destination and draws visitors keen to see magnificent wildlife from all corners of the globe. Big-game hunting expeditions, however, are now a thing of the past, and the only shooting of animals allowed today is with a camera. But even with the rigours of the bush eased by organised game drives and comfortable safari vehicles, little matches the sheer thrill of seeing your first herd of elephants or pride of lions in the wild.

If, on the other hand, you want nothing more demanding from your holiday than to lie under a palm tree, Kenya's coastline offers long stretches of unspoiled beach and fabulous coral reefs, interspersed with swish resorts.

A craft shop in the city market, Nairobi

The language

Kiswahili – the Swahili language – is a Bantu tongue whose vocabulary is an infusion of Arabic, Asian and European words. It is the *lingua franca* of Kenya and Tanzania, and is also spoken in several neighbouring countries.

Cultural Diversity

Home to more than 40 tribes, each with its own language, Kenya's national heritage is a patchwork quilt of different history and customs, sewn together by the colonial threads of the late 19th and early 20th centuries. This cultural diversity is one of Kenya's greatest assets, but also presents one of its most formidable social and political challenges. Surprisingly, perhaps, the tribes are formations that rarely go back more than a couple of hundred years and were sustained as elements of colonial administration at a time when they were progressively merging and dissolving.

The people of Kenya fall into three main linguistic groups: Bantu, Nilotic and Cushitic. Bantu-speakers, who make up about 70 percent of the population, speak languages rooted in the Congo Basin, while Nilotic- and Cushitic-speakers are migrants from further north. The Bantu-speaking Kikuyu of the central highlands are the largest population group, comprising nearly a quarter of the population; they enjoy considerable prestige and influence, despite efforts to lessen their dominance. They are followed by the Luo, from the shores of Lake Victoria, who make up another 10 percent; followed by the Luhya, the Kalenjin and the Kamba.

Kenya's most famous tribe is the Maasai, a group of tall pastoral nomads who tend to resist modern influences. They guard their cattle herds with spears and wear their traditional red cloaks and bright beaded jewellery.

Asians, Arabs and Europeans form small but vital minorities. The Indo-Pakistani communities who emigrated here during colonial times retain control over much of the country's retail businesses. Arab residents go back much further to the Swahili coastal settlements founded in the Middle Ages. Kiswahili is the *lingua franca* that ties them all together, though English is also an official language.

The land once ruled by the Europeans has been largely returned to African hands. But the colonial legacy is marked by the prevalence of the English language, customs and, for want of a better word, cuisine. Vehicles drive on the left, and the structure of government and public services all show the abiding influence of British models.

With an estimated population of 41 million, half of whom are under the age of 15, Kenya has one of the highest rates of population growth in the world. Yet only about one quarter of the land is arable. With this equation, poverty threatens to become more visible and more widespread. Yet, despite this, Kenya's social problems are not glaringly apparent.

Maasai dancing

School children in Lamu

What will strike you instead is the friendliness and easy-going nature of the people. Outside the larger cities there is a genuine interest in visitors and delight in casual chat. All along the road children wave, and even adults will often raise a hand in greeting.

Ups and Downs

Kenya is seen as an oasis of calm and stability on a continent whose post-colonial era is often associated with less desirable attributes. This image has been a great advantage in attracting the tourist trade; indeed, tourism has become one of the mainstays of the economy, with tea, coffee and horticulture, being the major foreign income earners. But recently, cracks have appeared in this veneer.

Much of the country's stability has been maintained through iron-handed rule. Much anticipated multi-party elections held in December 2002 brought about a landslide victory for Mwai Kibaki and his National Rainbow Coalition (NARC), giving Kenya a new ruling party for the first time since independence. However, while this result was widely welcomed, the contested December 2007 elections, which officially but controversially went in Kibaki's favour, with his main rival Raila Odinga trailing by only 3 percent, led to a short-lived but brutal outbreak of ethnic violence in which 800 people died. Peace was restored following negotiations that led to the formation of a Unity Government in April 2008, with Kibaki serving as President and Odinga as Prime Minister.

Other threats come from outside Kenya's borders. The conflicts in neighbouring Somalia and Sudan, for instance, have periodically spilt over into northern Kenya, usually in the form of occasional bandit attacks and an influx of refugees. Most recently, the 2011 famine in war-torn southern Somalia resulted in hundreds of thousands of refugees flooding into northern Kenya, while Kenya itself invaded Somalia in October of the same year following several kidnappings by the insurrectionary terrorist organisation Al-Shabaab. Outbreaks of poaching, though largely eliminated, sometimes flare up in the game parks. While these occurrences seldom endanger the casual tourist, always follow the advice of the authorities when travelling in remote regions, and respect any no-go areas. That said, when you go to Kenya, be prepared for an exciting sensory experience. You will have a trip here as you have never had before, and you'll also come back keener, more alive and more demanding of your usual surroundings.

Kilimanjaro

Except for the beginnings of its northern foothills, Kilimanjaro is entirely inside Tanzania, but the awe-inspiring view of it from Amboseli makes it an undeniable part of Kenya's landscape. At 5,895m (19,342ft), this vast dormant volcano is Africa's highest mountain. It has three great peaks: the highest is the snow-covered table known as Kibo, called Uhuru (freedom) since Tanzania gained independence; the western peak, Shira, is 4,005m (13,140ft); the eastern peak is Mawenzi, 5,150m (16,897ft) high, but tougher to climb than Kibo. Legend has it that the son of King Solomon and the Queen of Sheba, King Menelik of Abyssinia, also made it to the top. In heroic battles he conquered all of East Africa and then, as death approached, he climbed Kibo. He disappeared into the crater with his slaves, who carried his treasures, including Solomon's ring. Find that ring and you'll inherit Solomon's wisdom and Menelik's courage.

A BRIEF HISTORY

Man's earliest roots most probably lie in East Africa. Kenya – together with neighbouring Ethiopia and Tanzania – has yielded a large number of fossils charting the evolutionary path of humans since it diverged with that of the apes 6–8 million years ago. Key Kenyan finds include the arboreal *Orrorin tugenensis*, which lived about 6 million years ago and was unearthed in the Tugen Hills in 2000, and the oldest known Australopithecus fossils from the Lake Turkana region. In addition, stone tools associated with *Homo erectus* have been found in Kenya at sites on Rusinga Island, Hyrax Hill, Kariandusi and Olorgesailie, some dating back more than a million years.

Kenya's earliest societies were hunter-gatherers. Cattle-herding and agriculture emerged only *c*.1000BC. In fact, Kenya seems to have remained largely at a Stone Age level until *c*.AD1000, when signs of iron-smelting appeared, brought by Bantu-speaking tribes from the west and south. The gradual change from a hunting-and-gathering society to one of agriculture led to rapid increases in population in the fertile areas of the highlands and the grazing plateaux of the southwest.

Settlement of the Coast

Arabs landed on the Kenya coast in the 7th century AD, looking to develop trade between East Africa and the Far East. Later, the rise of Islam in the Middle East caused a wave of migration to the coastal strip – a pattern that continued into the 12th century. The intermingling of these settlers from the Persian Gulf with the local population gave rise to the emergence of Kiswahili – a Bantu language with some Arabic influences – as the *lingua franca* of coastal trade. Swahili was Kenya's first written language, as indicated by the Arabic characters inscribed on several mediaeval tombs. Swahili culture was also affected by interaction with Asia and the Far East.

Over the next 300 years, the Swahili trading centres, scattered along the coastline, developed into powerful city-states, of which Mombasa, Malindi and Lamu were the most important in Kenya. They produced iron and ceramics and traded with ships from Persia, India and the Far East, exchanging animal skins, ivory, tortoiseshell, gums and spices for sugar, grain and cloth. In 1498 Vasco da Gama, searching for a sea route to India, landed in Malindi. The Portuguese soon returned to plunder the rich coastal cities. While Mombasa fiercely resisted the encroachment, the Portuguese formed a trading alliance with its rival state, Malindi. Mombasa was attacked three times in the 16th century before being surrendered to the Portuguese in 1592.

Fort Jesus, Mombasa

From their new military garrison at Fort Jesus the Portuguese reigned for the next century, but repeated attacks by disaffected locals weakened their hold, as did threats to their position elsewhere in the Indian Ocean and the Gulf. In 1660 the Sultan of Oman supported a major revolt on Pate Island, north of Lamu. The Portuguese occupants were finally driven out of Mombasa in 1698.

Aided by British naval technology, the Omanis

suppressed the Swahili rebellions and became the new foreign overlords on the coast. Ruling from Zanzibar, they cultivated the ivory trade with the interior; then, in the 1830s, a new trade, slavery, proved more lucrative. By 1854 it had crossed over Kenya's borders into Uganda. Slavery was officially forbidden in 1873, but it took 20 years for the illegal trade to cease.

The Interior in the Late 19th Century

Prior to British colonisation, the East African interior was populated by a variety of Bantu-, Nilotic- and Cushitic-speaking peoples, whose languages originated with migrants from elsewhere in Africa. In some cases, these migrations dated back thousands of years, in other only a few hundred. Over the centuries, hunter-gather lifestyles were gradually replaced by agriculture and pastoralism, with the former tending to dominate in high rainfall areas, and the latter in more arid regions.

The Maasai and Samburu, who speak a Nilotic language called Maa, were probably the last ethnic group to arrive in Kenya. Gradually moving southward, within a few generations these obscure nomads had expanded along the plains and throughout the Rift Valley, to eventually become a strong force from Lake Turkana to Mount Kilimanjaro. Differences between Maasai groups erupted in the Maasai Civil Wars in the last half of the 19th century.

Political organisation varied greatly among these ethnic groups. The Bantu-speakers of northwest Kenya had a reasonably centralised society, with a council of elders advising a clan leader paid for his services in meat, grain or beer. But the eastern Bantu-speakers – most prominently the Kikuyu – were organised in peer groups known as age-sets, each serving a military, political or judicial function in ruling the tribal lands. Solidarity came through kinship and territorial allegiance, rather than loyalty to a central council of chief.

Swahili and Arab caravans from Mombasa ventured into the interior on ivory safaris, trading mainly with the Kamba tribe. The quality of ivory from Africa's elephants was considered superior to that of their Indian cousins and sold better in the Orient. The caravans opened up routes from Mombasa to Kilimanjaro, across the Rift Valley to Lake Victoria and even as far north as Lake Turkana. From the early 19th century onwards, the caravans became less interested in ivory and were more likely to return to the coast with a cargo of captive villagers, who would be sold on to plantation owners from the Indian Ocean islands at the slave market on Zanzibar.

Mt Kenya – the second highest mountain in Africa

Missionaries and adventurers from Britain and Germany had moved upcountry as early as 1846, laying the groundwork for later colonisation. Two of them, Johann Ludwig Krapf and Johann Rebmann, located Mounts Kenya and Kilimanjaro; another – John Hanning Speke – 'discovered' Lake Victoria in 1858, whilst Joseph Thompson explored Maasai territory in 1883. When the Europeans carved up the continent, Kenya, Uganda and Zanzibar went to the British, and Tanganyika (Tanzania) to the Germans. Each monarch got a snow-capped peak: Mount Kenya for Queen Victoria and Mount Kilimanjaro for Kaiser Wilhelm.

A 1929 poster promoting trade between Kenya and Britain

Under the Union Jack

The British colonised Kenya almost as an afterthought. They were, in fact, far more interested in their prospects in Zanzibar and Uganda. For several years, they left Kenya to the administration of the Imperial British East Africa Company (est. 1888), which imposed taxes, built trading posts and pursued the ivory trade in the interior. Inept management of the territory forced the British government to take over the operation of what it called the 'East Africa Protectorate' seven years later.

A means of transport was needed between the coast and the source of the River Nile to reduce costs and develop plantation agriculture. In 1896 construction began on a railway line to connect Mombasa with Port Florence, today's Kisumu, which was later extended into Uganda. To pay for the high cost of the project, the government publicised the previously remote highlands as a great farming and settlement region. Immigrants from Britain, Europe and South Africa flooded in.

Lord Delamere, a pioneer agriculturalist, became champion of the white settlers. In 1903 he was given a grant of 40,000ha (98,840 acres) of rich farmland in the central highlands, north of Nairobi. Other settlers also appropriated huge landed estates for themselves, and introduced coffee, tea and pineapples.

Cereals and other European crops also thrived, and this fertile region soon became known as the 'White Highlands'.

Within a few years, half of the prime farmland was controlled by the settlers. The Kikuyu were driven out and resettled on native reserves, where the growing population faced grave land shortages. Many had no choice but to work for the settlers as farm labourers and domestic servants. Colonial authorities imposed control by appointing tribal chiefs to collect hut taxes. A new class structure developed, as young Africans competed for wealth and privileges conferred by these chieftainships. One of the most hated laws required Africans to register and carry ID cards.

Apart from Swahili towns on the coast, Kenya's urban areas were all European in origin. Africans could work but not live there, except as 'sojourners' in shanty towns on the outskirts. Indians as well as Africans were denied farming rights in the White Highlands. In 1907 the capital of the protectorate was shifted from Mombasa to Nairobi, which had been founded less than a decade earlier as a camp along the railway line to Lake Victoria. It was not until 1920 that the region became known as the Crown Colony of Kenya, a name derived from the country's highest peak.

African Ascendency

World War I had a profound effect on the 200,000 African soldiers who were conscripted into the British army. Living and fighting side by side in the campaign for Tanganyika, Kenyans learned military tactics and witnessed at first hand the white man's real strengths and weaknesses. At the end of the war, the Soldier Resettlement Scheme rewarded the white servicemen with new land rights, while Kenyans returned to impoverished living conditions. This caused great bitterness, and political activist groups sprang up, made up chiefly of Kikuyu ex-soldiers.

The strongest group was the East African Association, led by a government clerk named Harry Thuku. At the peak of the protests in 1921, Thuku was arrested and imprisoned for 11

Jomo Kenyatta dressed as an extra for *Sanders of the River*

years. Other militant groups, such as the Kikuyu Central Association (KCA), carried on the nationalist movement. It was known as Uhuru: the call for independence.

In the 1920s and 1930s, settlers in the White Highlands enjoyed an unprecedented heyday of good fortune. Meanwhile, the government tried to diffuse the clamour for independence by courting the more moderate among the African leaders. In 1944 Eliud Mathu was made the first African member of Kenya's Legislative Council. Moreover, he was also permitted to form an advisory group.

Just two years later, Jomo Kenyatta, one of the movement's first leaders, returned to Nairobi after 16 years of study and political activism in England. He took over Mathu's advisory group, renamed it the Kenya African Union, and set about transforming the small educated elite into a mass political movement open to all workers and war veterans.

However, differences grew between Kenyatta's radicals – who sought independence through revolutionary methods – and the moderates surrounding Eliud Mathu, who wanted a reformist approach. The moderates especially resented Kikuyu domination of the KAU, and Kenyatta agreed that multi-tribal leadership was essential to national independence, a problem that plagued him after independence was achieved.

The Mau Mau

An underground movement arose when Kikuyus took secret oaths against the British government, sparking guerilla attacks against settlers in the White Highlands. The Mau Mau rebellion is believed to have been named after a Kikuyu warning that the enemy was coming. A state of emergency was declared in 1952, and though the KAU did not participate in the attacks, Kenyatta and other leaders were jailed.

The fighting was fierce. Thousands of Kikuyu, Embu and Meru civilians were resettled in guarded areas. In 1956, British troops drove the Mau Mau bands into the Mount Kenya and Aberdare forests, where they were killed or captured. The casualties of the rebellion numbered over 11,000 Mau Mau, 2,000 African civilians, 50 British troops and 95 European settlers.

The armed rebellion was broken, but colonial authority was at an end. In 1960 the White Highlands, covering 800,000ha (1,976,840 acres), were opened up to black ownership.

However, Kenya's tribal conflicts remained unresolved, as the Kikuyu-dominated Kenya African National Union (KANU)

Out of Africa

A casualty of the early 20th century was the first Baroness (Karen) Blixen, whose hunter husband, Bror, went off with another woman and left her to go bankrupt on a suburban Nairobi coffee farm under the Ngong Hills. Her memoir, *Out of Africa* – remarkable for its stylish insight on the country and people – was eloquent on the since exaggerated and romanticised high life of Kenya in the 1920s and 1930s. She entertained Edward, Prince of Wales, and had her own romantic interlude with a raffish member of the club, the Hon. Denys Finch Hatton. But the overall impression was that of a slightly desperate gaiety, rather like that of pre-Revolutionary Russia in *The Cherry Orchard*. The peasant revolution, in the form of the Kikuyu independence movement, was close at hand.

competed for power with the Kenya African Democratic Union (KADU) of the minority tribes. Jomo Kenyatta returned from exile to lead KANU in 1961. Independence was finally achieved on 12 December 1963, and, when a republic was proclaimed the next year, Kenyatta was named president.

Independence

Kenyatta began his presidency under the banner of Harambee: 'pulling together'. His skill in transferring power to African hands, while courting the aid and support of the former colonial rulers, earned him the title of respect, Mzee, or 'Honourable Old Man', while Kenya emerged as a model of democracy and progress among African countries.

The KADU opposition was dissolved and Kenya became a one-party state. There was growing corruption and internal unrest, but political dissent was squashed by persecution and the fear generated by the assassination of Tom Mboya, a Luo politician tipped to become the next president. Kikuyu dominance grew and Kenyatta died one of the world's richest men in 1978.

Daniel arap Moi, a member of the minority Kalenjin tribe, was chosen to succeed Kenyatta in order to combat tribal rivalry between the Kikuyu and the Luo. His initial efforts to wipe out tribalism and corruption were well received but short-lived. The next decade was marred by an attempted military coup in August 1982, accusations of internal plots against the government, student unrest and human-rights violations.

In the early 1990s Western donors, alarmed at reports of widespread corruption and political repression, suspended further aid until the Moi government demonstrated progress on human rights and political reform. As a result, in late December 1992, Kenya held its first multi-party elections since independence. The opposition parties that emerged were unable to form a united block to unseat Moi, who was re-elected amid accusations of vote-rigging and ethnic clashes in the provinces.

However, Kenyans continued to strive for stability, growth and prosperity. Elections were held in 1997, but again the opposition parties were not strong enough to defeat KANU. In the late 1990s the IMF imposed a three-year freeze on funds – a block that finally ended in July 2000. A new poverty reduction and growth facility was agreed upon, but this failed on the grounds of the government not meeting its commitments on governance.

In 2001 Moi appointed Raila Odinga and three members of the National Development Party (NDP) and set the stage for the first coalition government in Kenya's post-independent history. KANU merged with the NDP in early 2002, with Moi finally picking Uhuru Kenyatta to succeed him. The Rainbow Alliance was then formed, comprising former NDP members in KANU and other KANU members. This Rainbow Alliance formally broke away from KANU and transformed itself into the Liberal Democratic Party (LDP) and merged with Ford-People to form the National Rainbow Coalition (NARC). In the December 2002 Presidential elections, Mwai Kibaki won a landslide victory, as did NARC, bringing into power a new ruling party for the first time since independence.

In November 2002 an Islamic terrorist bomb at the Paradise Hotel near Mombasa killed 13 people, illustrating the weakness of

Celebrations on Mashujaa (Heroes') Day

Kenya's security. In 2003 there were further security warnings when commercial flights from the UK were suspended for six weeks. Since then, major players in the industry have promoted Kenya tourism overseas. The country is now reaping the benefits with major bookings in hotels and lodges.

Kenya's young democracy suffered its biggest setback when, shortly after the presidential elections of 2007, it was officially announced that Mwai Kibaki, standing for the Party of National Unity, had defeated Raila Odinga of the Orange Democratic by a margin of 3 percent. The result was expected to go the other way and was widely disputed, leading to a wave of civil unrest. At least 800 people died in the violence, and an estimated 600,000 were displaced as a result of it.

Fortunately, the crisis proved to be short lived. Negotiations led to the installation of a Unity Government in April 2008, with Mwai Kibaki retaining the Presidency but Raila Odinga serving alongside him as Prime Minister. The coalition held firmer than might have been expected, with the same two men still holding power at the start of 2012.

In October 2011, Kenyan troops invaded neighbouring Somalia in pursuit of Al-Shabaab, the Islamic terrorist organisation blamed for a series of tourist murders and kidnappings in northeast Kenya. This invasion, backed by the Somali government, is still ongoing at the time of writing, and while the signs are that Al-Shabaab is in retreat, it is questionable whether it can be eliminated entirely from the East African political scene.

Embassy bombing memorial, Nairobi

Historical Landmarks

1.8 million BC Ancestral hominids living on the shores of Lake Turkana.
AD500,000 Cushitic, Nilotic and Bantu peoples move into Kenya.
c.900 Arrival of Islam, marking the beginning of the coast's golden age.
14th century Swahili community emerges.
1498 Vasco da Gama arrives in Malindi.
1583 Portuguese begin construction of Fort Jesus in Mombasa.
1699 Omani Arabs capture Fort Jesus. Portugal withdraws.
1824 Kenya claimed as a British Protectorate.
1886 Kenya and Uganda are assigned to the British.
1921 Harry Thuku arrested. Protesting Kenyans massacred in Nairobi.
1944 Start of Mau Mau rebellion.
1952 Simmering Kenyan nationalism leads to attacks against white settlers. Kenyatta and other leaders imprisoned.
1959 Kenyatta released and put under house arrest.
1963 Kenya gains independence; Kenyatta is first elected president.
1964 Kenya declared a republic.
1978 Daniel Toroitich arap Moi becomes president on death of Kenyatta.
1982 Attempted coup by rebels in the Kenyan Air Force is put down.
1992 First multi-party elections for 26 years are held. Moi is re-elected.
1993 Economic crisis: Kenyan shilling devalued by around 50 percent.
1997 Moi is re-elected president.
1998 Islamic terrorist car bomb near US Embassy in Nairobi kills over 200.
2002 13 killed in Mombasa terrorist attack. Mwai Kibaki elected.
2003 Government introduces free primary education.
2005 Kenyan electorate rejects new draft constitution in a referendum.
2007 Riots break out as Kibaki's election victory is called into question.
2008 Kibaki and rival Raila Odinga form a stable Unity Government.
2010 East African Common Market allows for free trade between Kenya, Burundi, Rwanda and Tanzania.
2011 Uhuru Kenyatta questioned about post-election violence. Famine forces 400,000 Somalis to flee for refugee camps in Kenya. Kenya invades Somalia in pursuit of Al-Shabaab insurgents blamed for Kenyan kidnappings.

WHERE TO GO

Kenya's major cities, the modern capital Nairobi and ancient seaport of Mombasa, are cosmopolitan and well connected centres. Elsewhere, however, much of Kenya possesses a wild and timeless quality, when it comes to both the landscapes and the wildlife, which backtrack in time, following the millennia down to primal Lake Turkana, which is steeped in fossils evoking the origins of man. The remains of times long past are evident across the country. Immediately northwest of Nairobi, the Great Rift Valley is pockmarked with massive volcanoes associated with ancient geological upheavals. The sentinel Mount Kenya stands over the agricultural heartland of the country. The Age of the Mammals is evident all over Kenya, but exemplified in dozens of national parks and other private and public reserves, where the animals and pristine landscapes are entirely conserved.

National Parks and Game Reserves

Kenya's most celebrated monuments are not cathedrals, palaces or other human creations, but the great herds of wildlife that naturally roam the length and breadth of the country. Within the country's national parks and reserves, animals are accorded a privileged position, and are protected against the wanton hunting and poaching that took a heavy toll on wildlife in the colonial era, and more recently in the 1980s, when rhino and elephant in particular were targeted by commercial poaching cartels. Since 1989, however, the Kenya Wildlife Service (KWS) has made great efforts to eliminate poaching and improve conditions and safety within the parks, enabling visitors to a network of conservation areas comprising 7 percent of the country's total land area.

Reticulated giraffes in Laikipia

Protecting Kenya's wildlife is no small task. The parks are under intense pressure both from commercial developers and the growing population. Soil, trees and other vegetation that make up the ecosystem must also be conserved for the animals to survive. Most parks in Kenya are not fenced, allowing game to migrate freely back and forth through transitional zones, but this natural order is becoming increasingly threatened as man and beast compete for the land and its resources.

KWS has begun a number of community wildlife programmes, whereby a portion of the gate takings at the parks is set aside for development projects in the adjacent areas, thereby enabling the local communities to see a direct benefit from wildlife conservation.

Kenya's national parks do not stop at the water's edge. A coral reef runs along nearly the entire length of the coast, and several marine national parks and reserves have been established

Ecotourism

This is a growing market in Kenya: an increasing number of ranches and local communities are offering safari holidays that preserve and foster both the wildlife and the culture in their area. To raise funds for conservation and social projects, they build small lodges using local materials, and staff them with trained personnel from the area. The fees are used for local projects – schools, dispensaries, water supply – which also provide employment. These lodges are often in stunning locations, with a wide scope for exploring, game drives, walks and birdwatching.

Many of these community-run eco-lodges are to be found in the Laikipia/Samburu region, including Il Ngwesi, Tassia, Borana and the Lewa Wildlife Conservancy. Namunyak is slightly further north in the Mathews Range, while Porini Camps operates a trio of small tented camps on the same principle on private Maasai conservancies close to Amboseli National Park and the Maasai Mara.

to preserve this fascinating underwater ecosystem of live corals, tropical fish and other marine animals.

Safaris – a Swahili word meaning 'journey' – are organised into the bush in four-wheel-drive vehicles and minibuses with pop-up roofs that allow wildlife viewing and photography at close quarters. Just after sunrise and late afternoon are the

Lesser flamingos at Lake Oliedon

best times for a game drive, before and after the animals settle down to rest in the heat of the day.

Game spotting is definitely an acquired skill, and the services of a driver or guide are invaluable; he can take you to the places most likely to shelter the more elusive animals, and provide useful information and folklore about the animals' habits. Keep on the lookout: animals have a natural camouflage, and without an experienced pair of eyes you may never notice that cheetah sinking slowly into the tall grass.

On safari, you will have many opportunities for photographing and filming wildlife, or simply viewing it with binoculars, but remember that much of what you see is down to luck. When you read or hear about what species you can expect to see at this or that park, bear in mind that animals are seldom seen twice in the same place. Some species migrate, as weather conditions change and availability of food and water varies daily. During dry periods they tend to congregate around waterholes; after a rainy spell the vegetation is higher and denser, making the animals much harder to see. It's better to relax and enjoy whatever the luck of the safari brings your way. Most national parks and reserves are open to day visitors from sunrise to sunset (6am to 7pm) and overnight visitors are forbidden from driving outside camp and lodge grounds at other times. Walking in most parks and reserves is forbidden except at designated picnic sites, the exception being those such as Mount Kenya, Kakamega Forest and Arabuko-Sokoke, whose habitats are more suited to exploration on foot than by vehicle. For full details of all reserves that fall under the auspices of the Kenya Wildlife Service, see www.kws.org.

THE BIG FIVE

The idea of a 'Big Five' dates from the days when safaris were not so much about photographing and enjoying the wildlife than about shooting it for trophies. Inevitably, some creatures were regarded as more dangerous or desirable targets than others, reflecting the skill it took to track them, the risk involved in confronting them and the quality of the trophy retrieved from a successful kill. In time, five mammals that qualified on all counts were recognised as the ultimate objectives of a hunting safari: the buffalo, elephant, leopard, lion and black rhinoceros. Today, hunting is outlawed in Kenya but the Big Five still have their cachet.

Buffalo

The African buffalo, traditionally known as the meanest beast in the bush, is generally a very placid creature, but single males in particular will occasionally launch a charge without obvious warning or provocation, and any buffalo is dangerous when wounded. As grazers, buffalos are generally found in grassland, where they do most of their feeding and moving around in the evening, night and early morning. Buffalos, which weigh up to 800kg (1,750lb), must drink daily, so are never found more than 15km (9 miles) from water. Like domestic cattle, they probably sleep for no more than an hour a day.

Buffalos live in herds of relatively stable size. They may number up to 2,000, but large herds tend to fragment during the dry season and regroup in the wet. This spreads the grazing load when grass is in short supply. Bachelor groups of 10 to 15 are common, and consist either of old, retired bulls who no longer bother to keep competing for females, or younger bulls nearing their prime. Solitary old males or small bull groups are the animals most likely to charge intruders.

Elephant

Although the lion has long been regarded as the king of beasts, when you see an elephant herd working out its own hierarchy in nature, you are likely to conclude that it is the supreme monarch. An adult male, 3m (10ft) tall, often weighs over 5,400kg (11,905lb) and each tusk may weigh up to 90kg (198lb). The female, just under 3m, weighs a mere 3,500kg (7,700lb). But it

A buffalo at the Soysambu Conservancy

African elephants

is the females who do all the work, are the leaders of herds and group their own baby and adolescent offspring and that of their daughters. Male elephants are chased away from the herd as soon as they are old enough to fend for themselves (12 to 14 years) and join up with other males.

Enormously affectionate, female elephants also do all the fighting to protect their young from lions and hyenas. The males turn up only when one of the females goes into heat. Pregnancy lasts up to 22 months, the longest of any mammal. Living till a grand old age of 50 to 60 years, elephants are known to bury their own dead and indeed other dead animals, even dead human beings they have killed: but, contrary to legend, they do not have mass burial grounds.

Leopard

The leopard is always – and justifiably – described as elusive, making it the most desirable of the Big Five to many experienced safari-goers, and any sighting should be regarded as a stroke of good fortune. Leopards keep to the cover of trees or dense under-growth and their solitary, stealthy habits enable them to survive the attention of poachers much better than lions and cheetahs.

Females seem to roam at will, while male leopards are definitely territorial, staking out their home range by spray-ing urine along the boundaries and fighting off other males who might trespass. The big feline's usual roar sounds like wood sawing, but during mating it turns into a snarling and caterwauling reminiscent of alley cats, only around ten times louder. Unlike cheetahs, the females make very affectionate mothers and continue to meet up with their offspring, even after they've grown up and left home.

Leopards, like cats, are nocturnal beasts, spending the day resting in the shade, either under an overhanging hillside rock or up a tree, anywhere, in fact, where they can survey the surrounding countryside. Weighing between 35 and 55kg (75 and 120lb) on average, they are powerful and versatile hunters, prepared to kill anything from small birds to animals as much as three times their size. Leopards can carry up to 45kg (100lb) of uneaten meat into the higher branches of a tree, out of the reach of scavengers. They particularly enjoy eating other carnivores such as foxes, jackals and serval cats, among others. This accounts for their notorious partiality for domestic dogs on occasions when they have wandered into town.

Leopard in Meru National Park

Lion

The lion is the largest, the most impressive and the most feared of African predators. It is also the only truly sociable species among the world's 40 felids, typically living in prides comprising up to 20 individuals. These are often made up of several small families spread over a wide area, but they are still more loosely knit groups than elephant herds. Lions roam over a territory that covers perhaps as much as 50sq km (some 20sq miles) in groups of threes and

fours, usually lionesses with their cubs, while male lions tend to roam together, keeping separate from the females until mealtime.

Lions are ferocious hunters, but in the daylight hours when you will see them, they are more likely to seem docile, lazy, imperturbable and even downright amiable. Unless, of course, they were unable to find a meal during the night, in which case their hunger might rouse them into action. A male attached to a pride will leave almost all the hunting to the females; only when the kill has been made will it throw around its weight (240kg/528lb compared to the female's 150kg/330lb), and fight off the lionesses and cubs to take the lion's share. In the male's defence, we can only say that his presence as a sentinel does keep the pride area safe for the lioness and her cubs.

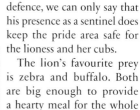

Lions at the Maasai Mara National Reserve

The lion's favourite prey is zebra and buffalo. Both are big enough to provide a hearty meal for the whole family, but also strong enough, especially buffalo, to require group effort for a kill. Most antelopes can be knocked off single-handedly.

Lions are extremely sensuous beasts. They like to lick, groom and rub up against each other, often as an act of group solidarity before the hunt or just out of good fellowship during the after-dinner siesta. Male lions are especially vain about grooming their opulent mane, their chief sexual selling-point. The roar, heard most often before dawn or early evening, is a crescendo of deep rolling grunts quite unlike that fabricated MGM groan.

Rhinoceros

Between 1970 and 1990, the number of rhinos in Kenya dwindled from at least 8,000 to a few hundred. Fortunately, increased protection since that poaching-induced nadir

White rhinoceros near Lake Nakuru

means the population probably now stands at more than 1,000, concentrated in Tsavo West, Lake Nakuru and Meru National Parks, along with the private conservancies of Laikipia. Both species of rhino – black and white – occur in Kenya, the former naturally, the latter introduced from South Africa.

Rhino tend to live alone, though groups of two and three (often including a mother and her young) are sometimes seen. There is nothing more desolate than the screaming groan of a solitary rhino disturbed by another at his waterhole. However, there is one creature that can approach the rhino with impunity: the little oxpecker, which perches on the rhino's back. In exchange for the rhino's ticks and flies, the oxpecker provides a loudly chattering alarm system to warn the sleeping rhino of any approaching danger.

Mother rhinos are ferocious defenders of their young. A concerted attack by three male lions on a rhino calf can result in one of the lions being killed and the other two slinking away. The rhino can move his 2,000+kg (4,400lb) bulk up to 55kph (35mph), at least as fast as a lion, with an amazing ability to wheel suddenly to face an attack from the rear.

There's nothing remotely delicate about rhinos, not even their copulating, which is accompanied by ferocious snorting and jousting resistance from the female before she submits. Unlike the few seconds expended by most animals, copulation between rhinos lasts more than 30 minutes, and this is thought to account for the mythic properties attributed to that horn.

OTHER PREDATORS

The predators in the 'Big Five' are not the only animals to live by hunting and killing; others include cheetahs, smaller cats, dogs, jackals, foxes, mongooses, genets and civets.

Cheetah

Cheetahs are not very gregarious, often hunting alone and so unable to protect their kill when attacked by scavenging lions, hyenas or even vultures. A mother will dutifully rear her cubs and then part quite abruptly from them. They never acknowledge each other again. Male cheetahs either fend for themselves or operate in coalitions of two or three brothers, meeting up with females exclusively for mating – and then only after a fierce fight.

The mother's training of her cubs for hunting is a careful affair, as would befit the fastest mammal on earth: an amazing 112kph (70mph). At first, the mother cheetah makes the kill herself, usually by biting through the prey's windpipe. The cub picks up the dead prey by the throat and 'strangles' it again. Gradually, the mother lets the growing cub have first go at catching the prey, and only if he botches it will she intervene, so as not to risk totally losing the meal. Alternatively, the mother makes the first thrust and then leaves the weakened prey for the cub to finish off. When he reaches 14 months, the cub is considered ready to do the job alone. You have a fair chance of seeing a cheetah kill, since it is the only African felid that routinely hunts by day.

Hyena

With their oversized heads, sloped backs, scruffy fur and clumsy gait, hyenas are not the most appealing creatures. They also have a dozen ways to make a horrible din and a miserable reputation as cowardly scavengers. But field studies have revealed hyenas to resort much more to hunting than scavenging for their food. They hunt with considerable intelligence and courage, even attacking rhinoceroses and young elephants. Lions are stronger than hyenas; they often steal the latter's kill and rely more on scavenging than the much-maligned hyena.

A cheetah at Ol Pejeta Wildlife Conservancy

Grouped in tightly knit clans of up to 20 members, they live in a den with entrance holes connected by a network of tunnels. They mark out the clan territory with their dung and go on regular border patrols to keep out rival clans. Unusual among the mammals, the females are stronger and heavier than the males (70kg to the male's 58kg: 154 to 128lb). This evolution is thought to result from the mother's need to protect her young against the male's frequent cannibalistic tendencies.

Clan solidarity is constantly reinforced, particularly before a hunt, with some elaborate meeting ceremonies: they will sniff each other's mouths, necks and heads, raise a hind leg and lick each other before going off, reassured, on the group activity. Hunting is a carefully co-ordinated affair.

GRAZERS AND BROWSERS

The grasslands and bushlands of East Africa support the finest variety of herbivores in the world. In Kenya alone, there are more than 30 different species of antelope, ranging in size from the eland – the world's largest antelope – to the tiny Ader's duiker. Some antelope graze (eat grass) indiscriminately; others graze selectively, choosing their habitat according to their diet; others graze and browse (eat the shoots and leaves of trees and shrubs); and a few are almost exclusively browsers.

Whatever they eat, all antelopes are ruminants – that is, they have several stomachs for fodder in varying stages of digestion and they reprocess already swallowed fodder by chewing the cud, like buffalos and domestic cattle.

All species are diurnal (active in the day), with a preference for mornings and evenings for feeding. Except for impala and some of the very small antelopes, most breed in a very narrow period, usually giving birth to their calves just before the rains. Antelopes rely on alertness and flight to escape their enemies – predators such as lions, leopards, cheetahs and hyenas.

Wildebeest

The rather ungainly-looking wildebeest has a dark brown/black body, an erect mane and a long whitish tail. Both sexes have horns, which are straight as calves, but forward-curving in the adult animal. Wildebeest are primarily grazers, found in herds. Their preferred habitat is open grassland, and they actively avoid areas with tall grass and dense vegetation, where they are very susceptible to being hunted. You are likely to see wildebeest in large numbers – possibly hundreds of thousands – if you visit the Maasai Mara when they are passing through on their annual migration between August and October. Watch out for them in single file as they make their dangerous path across the plains.

Giraffe

The giraffe has, it seems, achieved a state of grace, an ineffable dignity, just from being quite literally above it all – as much as 5m (16ft) for males. He relies on acute eyesight and his privileged vantage point to see potential dangers long before they arrive, fleeing instead of coping with them in a fight. The giraffe gets his liquid from juicy or dew-covered foliage, so as to avoid bending down to drink ground water in an ungainly split, vulnerable to attack from lions.

Giraffe at the Maasai Mara National Reserve

Females give birth standing up, and the calf, already almost 2m (6.5ft) tall and weighing 65kg (143lb), is dropped, head first and with a thud, over a metre to the ground. The fall breaks the umbilical cord.

Three types of giraffe occur in Kenya, and they are traditionally regarded as races of the same species, though recent DNA evidence suggests all three may be good species. The reticulated giraffe, found only in northern Kenya, is bronze coloured with a distinct web-like pattern to its coat; the Maasai giraffe, which is smaller and darker with a ragged spot pattern; and the Rothschild giraffe, the tallest and most endangered variety, has a coat pattern somewhere in between.

Zebra

The zebra herd consists of strong family units, in which a stallion stays together with up to six mares and their foals, and groups of male bachelors. The bachelor groups are quite frivolous, spending most of their time racing, wrestling and generally fooling around. Relations between the stallion and his 'harem' are cordial, enhanced by mutual grooming. Unlike many animals, the zebra stallion is friendly and courteous to other stallions in the herd. When lions or hyenas threaten, the stallion just stands his ground, biting and kicking the aggressors to give his family plenty of time to escape. This ploy is quite often successful because lions prefer to rely on surprise attack, rather than a pitched battle, for making their kill. The common zebra in Kenya is the Plains zebra, a widespread species whose range extends to South Africa, but the northern badlands around Samburu are the main global stronghold for the larger and more narrow-striped Grevy's zebra, an endangered species that is now close to extinction outside Kenya.

Zebra at Hell's Gate National Park

Hippopotomus

Man is the hippo's only real threat, although a pride of lions will attack a solitary hippo on land, and crocodiles take the occasional baby hippo in the water. Females defend their young by making use of their long tusks (actually canine teeth). Despite their benign look, hippos probably account for more wildlife-induced human deaths than any other animal, including lions and snakes. They specialise in capsizing boats which get too near, either drowning or biting the people inside. Hippos are also dangerous on land at night, since they will run over anybody standing between them and the water.

Monkey

Though not strictly vegetarian, East Africa's monkeys should be mentioned here. Several species live in Kenya, but most of them are localised in their distribution – the blue monkey, for instance, in small pockets in the west of the country; the De Brazza's monkey in forests on Mount Elgon and the Cherengani Range; the patas monkey in savannah country around Nanyuki, Rumuruti and Eldoret-Kitale; and the black-and-white colobus in highland forests.

One versatile monkey that is found throughout the country is the vervet (*Cercopithecus aethiops*), also known as the green, grivet and tantalus monkey. It is slight of build, agile and long-tailed, and always seen in noisy, bickering, family troops with lots of young animals. Both sexes are similar, although males are about 40 percent heavier, with conspicuous red, white and blue genital colouration.

Vervets generally inhabit well-wooded and well-watered grasslands but can also be found in semi-arid regions (usually near rivers or swamps) and evergreen forest edges at altitudes from sea level to 4,000m (13,000ft). They are diurnal animals, although they may feed on moonlit nights. They have acute eyesight and excellent hearing, but a poor sense of smell. As well as vocal calls, they have a range of facial expressions, such as lowering their eyebrows, baring their teeth, raising or jerking their head.

Vervets are very gregarious and live in troops of six to 60 animals, sometimes reaching as many as 100. Troops comprise one or more adult males, adult females and young of all ages

Grooming baboons

and sizes. Troops are territorial and defend their range against neighbouring troops with noisy group displays at the territory boundary.

Vervets are omnivorous with a predilection for vegetable matter. Their preferred tastes include fruits, flowers, grass seeds, shoots and bark, as well as insects, reptiles, small mammals, young birds and eggs.

Baboon

Behaviourists have used the baboon as an analogy for theorising about natural aggressiveness and male dominance among human beings. Quite apart from the dubious value of making such parallels, recent observations of baboons have shown them to be motivated not by fear and brutal tyranny, as had been claimed previously, rather by strong family relationships and social co-operation.

While the males play an important role in guaranteeing the safety of the baboon troop, it is the females who provide the group's stability. Females stay in the troop all their lives, while males are constantly on the move. Social cohesion is built around the family, with perhaps as many as 20 related units of mother and offspring. The males, for their part, form a separate band, moving on the outskirts of the group as it hunts for food.

You will often see male, female and baby baboons grooming each other. Their search for ticks, knots and dirt is an activity that reinforces group solidarity and what zoologists do not hesitate to call friendship. Male and female baboons form companionships independent of sexual mating. There is a definite hierarchy of prestige among female baboons, and the males seek some reflected glory by associating with the most prominent females – the troop's effective leaders who decide exactly when to move and which direction to take.

The baboons' diet consists of young shoots of savannah grass, shrubs and herbs, but their favourite food is fruit, especially figs. They occasionally turn carnivore and hunt down birds, hare and young gazelles. Indeed, nothing would be safe on an unguarded picnic.

BIRDS

The variety of birds in Kenya is more striking even than the range of mammals. From the tiny sunbirds to the ostrich (at up to 2.75m/9ft the world's biggest bird, as well as one of the fastest – running at up to 70kph or 45mph), the range is so diverse that more than 1,100 species have been recorded from all over the country, with several places boasting checklists of 500-plus. Savannah birds include the marabou stork, secretary bird, southern ground hornbill, vulturine guineafowl and African hoopoe, as well as various species of vulture, bustard, eagle, hawk, falcon, buzzard, oxpecker, lark and lapwing.

In addition, a variety of brightly coloured turacos, hornbills and robin-chats can

A vervet monkey at Lewa Wildlife Conservancy

be seen in the forests, while various storks, cranes, pelicans, flamingos, cormorants and ibises are plentiful near the lakes, along with the peculiar hamerkop and striking African fish eagle.

REPTILES

The richness of reptiles in East Africa compares favourably with any other part of the world. Reptiles have little commercial value in Kenya, so poaching is not a major problem. A few crocodiles are killed for their skins and smuggled out individually, but there is little trade in snakes and lizards. The Nile crocodile inhabits Kenya's rivers and lakes; it takes many human lives every year. Other reptiles to look out for include snakes such as the venomous mambas, adders and cobras, along with a variety of non-venomous species including the outsized pythons. Lizards include the house-dwelling geckos and colourful agamas.

Photography

Kenya's dramatic landscapes and awesome wildlife make it a photographer's heaven, and few people come without a camera. The safari vehicles and land cruisers have pop-up roofs to give you unimpeded standing shots while on game drives, although 'camera shake', from shooting from a moving vehicle, is common. A zoom of some kind is highly recommended for wildlife shots, otherwise, when you see your prints, you'll often find the animals have shrunk to the size of a pea. Most animals are shy and won't wait around to give you a perfect pose; the quickest photographer often gets the best shot.

People are another matter. Be sensitive to the various cultures you will come across; some tribes fear that a photo will capture their soul. Always ask permission before taking someone's photo, particularly Muslim women and tribes including the Maasai and Samburu. Some tribes will demand payment for posing.

NAIROBI

Central Nairobi

Founded little more than a century ago, Kenya's capital **Nairobi**  has grown from a remote railway outpost to become East Africa's largest city. Its modern skyline seems to announce its prominence as an international convention centre, a headquarters for multinational businesses and United Nations bureaux and, not least, the safari capital of the world. Kenya's political, administrative, business and trade activities are all centred on this town.

Nairobi has the attendant problems of capital cities everywhere: traffic, street crime and a rapidly growing population (estimated at around 3.2 million), many of whom are poor. But for thousands of visitors who pass through, preparing for the bush or resting up between safaris, the capital city is not

Boating on the lake in Uhuru Park, central Nairobi

Kenyatta International Conference Centre

an unpleasant place to be. At 1,660m (5,446ft) above sea level, Nairobi has an equatorial climate that is temperate all year round, with warm days and cool nights. There are plenty of restaurants, shops and service facilities and few mosquitoes.

In a country where hurry is not considered a virtue, the central streets of the city almost bustle. Most first-time visitors are unaware of the contrasts that lie between the shanty towns to the east and the landscaped homes of the northern and western suburbs. Instead, they notice the curious mixture of colonial legacy and African resurgence that makes up Nairobi.

In 1899, when builders of the Mombasa–Uganda railway line established a supply depot at Mile 327, the bleak, swampy riverside place that the Maasai called *enkare nyarobe* (sweet water) was nothing more than a campsite for hundreds of Indian labourers, and a few wooden shacks that housed the engineers who paused here to contemplate the difficulties of laying track across the Great Rift Valley. Soon, a frontier town emerged, with a central street (now Kenyatta Avenue) broad enough for a 12-span oxcart to wheel around.

Three years later the place was nearly abandoned when plague swept the town, and a government decree had it burned to the ground. Despite another plague in 1904,

Nairobi was rebuilt and by the time the Protectorate had offi-cially moved its headquarters there from Mombasa in 1907, the white hunters were streaming in to embark on safaris from the newly opened Norfolk Hotel. The most prominent of them was Theodore Roosevelt, the US President, who headed a safari with 500 porters, all dressed in blue, and each carrying 25kg (55lb) of supplies. In ten months – while out of office – Roosevelt bagged no less than 296 animals.

Meanwhile, the British government was strongly encourag-ing settlement of the Central Highlands, and Nairobi became the social and commercial centre for the growing white farm-ing community. Indian trad-ers developed the bazaar, while Africans came in from the villages to work as labourers. During World War II Nairobi served as a major garrison town, and much of the local game was killed to provide food for the troops. Thus, in 1947, the government formed the first of Kenya's many game sanctuaries, Nairobi National Park.

> **Meeting point**
>
> One of the traditional meeting places of Nairobi is the Fairmont Norfolk Hotel (see page 132), which you can enjoy even if you are staying elsewhere.

The building dominating the skyline, the **Kenyatta International Conference Centre Ⓐ**, symbolises the interaction of the city's European origins and African destiny by combining a cylindrical skyscraper with a cone-shaped congress hall, reminiscent of tribal huts. A **statue of Jomo Kenyatta**, the former freedom fighter who became the first president of Kenya at independence, sits alongside Garden Square, as do the old neoclassical Law Courts, the model of an English county court building.

White-columned arcades, the dominant architectural fea-ture of the business district, are perfectly adapted to the cli-mate, offering protection from the sudden rains or midday sun. They shelter the shops and restaurants along Mama Ngina Street – formerly Queensway and named after Kenyatta's wife – and Kimathi Street, named after Dedan Kimathi, a Mau Mau leader executed by the British in 1957.

The long, broad **Kenyatta Avenue** Ⓑ runs west from the Stanley. A few blocks north along Muindi Mbingu Street, a rather more African hub of activity can be found around the City Market. You can browse through fragrant flower and produce stalls in the main hall, but keep a tight hold on your valuables. The curio stands offer good bargains on soapstone, wood carvings and other handicrafts – if you can endure the overbearing stallholders. Across from the market is the Arabian-style Jamia Mosque, built in 1933 by the Sunni sect.

Situated on Museum Hill at the northern end of Uhuru Highway, the **Nairobi National Museum** Ⓒ (daily 9.30am–6pm; charge; www.museums.or.ke), which reopened in June 2008 following a major transformation, deserves a visit above all for its great prehistoric collection depicting the origins of man and various animals. On exhibition here is a replica of No. 1470, the skull belonging to our 2.5 million-year-old ancestor discovered at Lake Turkana. You can also view the findings from Olduvai Gorge in Tanzania: the fossilised 1.65 million-year-old remains of *Homo habilis*, the first tool-making man, with his stone hand-axes and cleavers; as well as *Homo erectus*, a 1.15-million-year-old man coming closer to the brain capacity of *Homo sapiens*.

The remains of prehistoric animals include a giant ostrich, rhinoceros and elephant; on a smaller scale are bird, insect and butterfly collections. In the courtyard is a stuffed model of Ahmed, the legendary elephant from Marsabit, who was declared a national monument by Kenyatta in 1970 and placed under 24-hour guard to protect him from poachers. He died of natural causes four years later, aged around 60, with each tusk weighing a mighty 67kg (148lb).

Across from the museum is the Snake House and aquariums, where you can safely view those creatures you hope never to see in the wild: the deadly green mamba, black mamba, puff adder and red spitting cobra.

City Outskirts

Whether or not you visit any of the country's more remote national parks and reserves, a day safari to **Nairobi National Park ❷** is highly recommended. True, the park's smooth well-marked roads may seem a little tame if you've already visited other parks, but it has a beautifully varied landscape of forest,

Nairobi National Museum

hills and savannah, and the sight of wildlife grazing against the backdrop of the city skyline is genuinely impressive.

There are lots of lions here, and the staff at the park entrance may tell you where they are to be found. While the park has no elephants, it does offer one of the best chances to see black and white rhino, both of which are quite common. Also look out for ostrich, warthog, baboon, zebra, giraffe and various antelope. Remarkably, although Nairobi National Park is fenced on the city side, it shares an open southern border with the Athi and Kaputei Plains, allowing the wildlife to migrate freely to and from Amboseli and Tsavo National Park.

At the western end of the park, the KWS Headquarters and main entrance gate is also the site of the **Nairobi Safari Walk**

National Independence Monument

and Animal Orphanage, which was founded in 1963 to provide a home for young animals injured or deserted in the wild. Zoologists who care for them until they can be returned to the reserves have a chance to study these animals up close. It's a good place for children to have their first easy look at Kenya's wildlife, but for adults it may seem little more than a glorified zoo.

En route to the park you will probably pass Kenya's majestic **National Independence Monument** in the Uhuru Gardens. It was erected on the site where the British government passed the papers of independence to the Kenyan people on 12 December 1963. A second monument marks the 25th anniversary of that day. And just off the Langata Road is another Nairobi institution, the **Carnivore Restaurant** (see page 106).

The **Bomas of Kenya** (Mon–Fri 2.30–4pm, Sat, Sun and public holidays 3.30–5.15pm; charge; www.bomasofkenya. co.ke), a few kilometres away, offers a chance to see a professional dance group perform a variety of Kenyan dance styles accompanied by traditional instruments you're unlikely to see elsewhere. The grounds are laid out with the traditional homesteads (bomas) of various tribes, and a selection of crafts is sold.

To meet orphaned elephants and rhinos up close, visit the **David Sheldrick Wildlife Trust** (daily 11am–noon; www. sheldrickwildlifetrust.org) situated just inside the Nairobi National Park through the Mbagathi Gate off the Magadi Road.

The nearby **AFEW Giraffe Centre**, on Koitobos Road off Langata South Road (daily 9.30am–5pm; charge; www.giraffecenter.org), was founded in 1978 as a breeding centre for Rothschild's giraffe, an endangered subspecies whose range is restricted to western Kenya and northern Uganda. Though the aim of the centre is to teach children about wildlife conservation, most adults enjoy the chance to hand-feed the giraffes as much as the kids do.

Another popular excursion is to the **Karen Blixen Museum** (daily 9.30am–6pm; charge; www.museums.or.ke) the homestead where the author (pen name Isak Dinesan) lived and ran her coffee farm from 1917 to 1931. After the grandeur of the Hollywood film *Out of Africa* (see page 21), which was shot here, the first thing that strikes you about the house is how small it is. The beautiful wood-panelled rooms have been restored and filled with original artefacts and reproductions. From the pretty gardens you can gaze over the Ngong Hills, where Karen Blixen's lover, Denys Finch Hatton, is buried.

Just northwest of the city centre is the suburb of Westlands with three shopping centres, assorted shops and a variety of restaurants offering international cuisine. Heading north of the city on Forest Road is Africa's first traditional Hindu Temple, **Shree Swaminarayan Mandir**, with intricate wooden and stone ceilings, pillars, walls and windows. On Limuru Road at Gigiri are the headquarters of the **United Nations**. A few minutes' drive from here is the **Village Market**, a shopping centre and leisure complex that is home to a popular Friday 'Maasai Market'.

THE CENTRAL HIGHLANDS

The Central Highlands, which lie to the north of Nairobi, are a fertile agricultural region whose highlights are the Aberdare National Park and Mount Kenya. In colonial days European settlers took much of the best land here for themselves, and the area became known as the 'White Highlands'. Today, however, the land is mostly farmed by the indigenous Kikuyu. The drive north from Nairobi is a pretty one, passing thatched huts, lush slopes of coffee trees and assorted horticultural produce. If you travel on a Tuesday or Saturday, stop by the open-air market at Karatina, about 20km (12 miles) before Nyeri, the centre of the region.

Aberdare National Park

The Aberdare Mountains, which form the steep eastern edge of the Rift Valley, were named after the Victorian president of the Royal Geographical Society, Lord Aberdare. The range is also known by its Kikuyu name 'Nyandarua', which means 'Drying Hide', supposedly a reference to its outline. This impressive range, an important water catchment for Nairobi and elsewhere, contains one of the country's largest protected forest areas and is rich in wildlife.

Due to the dense vegetation, it is not always easy to catch sight of the animals while driving through **Aberdare National Park ❸**. The best way to see them is to visit one of two purpose-built game-viewing lodges. Guests are driven from a base hotel in Nyeri or Mweiga (The Outspan for Treetops or Aberdare Country Club for the Ark) to the forest lodges, where they can watch the parade of wildlife around a watering hole.

Treetops, on the eastern edge of the park (see page 136), is the original 'tree hotel', literally built on stilts in a forest clearing. It started as a single cabin in 1932 for a few guests who would go there on moonlit nights to see the wild animals wander over to the waterhole and natural salt lick. Twenty years later, the hotel welcomed Princess Elizabeth and the Duke of Edinburgh as guests on their honeymoon. During their stay, news came of the death of King George VI and Elizabeth's ascension to the English throne. In 1954 Mau Mau rebels burned Treetops to the ground, but it was rebuilt three years later.

The peak of Mt Kenya at sunrise

The Ark, built to look like Noah's vessel, lies at a higher altitude in the middle of the forest. It is considered by many to be the better of the two lodges for game viewing; lions frequent the waterhole and the elusive leopard is occasionally sighted here.

North of Nyeri, on the **Laikipia Plateau ❹**, a different game-viewing experience awaits at a patchwork of private reserves that includes the Ol Pejeta Ranch, Solio Ranch and Lewa Wildlife Conservancy. All these private reserves specialise in night game drives, which are not allowed in Kenya's national parks, and the so-called Big Five are present throughout, with rhino being particularly common. Ol Pejeta also houses **Sweetwaters Chimpanzee Sanctuary**, whose inhabitants do not occur naturally in Kenya, but were translocated to what is the country's only ape sanctuary from an orphanage in Bujumbura during the civil war in Burundi.

Nyahururu

At 2,360m (7,742ft) **Nyahu-ruru ⑤** (Thompson's Falls) is Kenya's highest town, set almost on the equator. Its waterfall is named after the explorer Joseph Thompson, who discovered it in 1883. The falls are a popular stop-off point for tourists, though the 70m (230ft) cascade is pretty rather than dramatic, and the serenity

Thatched huts in Hamer village

of the surrounding forest is somewhat marred by the pestering of the curio sellers here. You can climb to the foot of the falls, but there is only one safe way down and it isn't easy to find. The best plan is to enquire at Thompson's Falls Lodge for a guide.

The **equator** is proclaimed by a yellow marker that states 'This Sign is on the Equator'. You'll no doubt be hassled by a 'guide' with a funnel and a bucket of water, who will demonstrate how water swirls clockwise down a drain north of the equator and anti-clockwise south of it.

Mount Kenya National Park

Africa's second highest mountain, **Mount Kenya**, in **Mount Kenya National Park ⑥** is an extinct volcano lying on the equator. The snow-capped twin peaks – Batian at 5,199m (17,058ft) and Nelion at 5,188m (17,022ft) – were named after two 19th-century Maasai ritual chiefs. Mount Kenya is the exponent of a remarkable natural phenomenon; the German missionary-explorer Johann Ludwig Krapf was mocked when he reported snowfields on the equator in 1849, but Joseph Thompson confirmed the phenomenon some 34 years later. In fact, Mount Kenya is the only point around the globe to have continuous equatorial snow.

The two highest peaks are regularly scaled by experienced climbers, though few make it to the top. A third peak, Lenana, at 4,985m (16,354ft) is known as 'Tourist Peak' because it is a relatively easy climb. The preferred entry point for a climb is Naro Moru, on the western side. The walk is a botanist's delight. The dense forest changes to bamboo jungle at 2,500m (8,200ft) and then, at 3,000m (9,840ft) to clearings surrounded by charming Abyssinian Hagenia trees hung with orchids, old-man's beard and several other creepers.

But there are much easier ways to enjoy Mount Kenya, with the **Serena Mountain Lodge** (see page 135) lying at the southwestern edge of the massif inside Mount Kenya National Park and offering the best spot for game viewing.

A view of Mt Kenya

The **Mount Kenya Safari Club** (see page 135) is a luxurious landmark on the mountain's northwest foothills. If you can't splurge on a night here, treat yourself to the buffet lunch and marvel at this equatorial oasis set against the mountain backdrop. You can also visit the adjacent **Mount Kenya Wildlife Conservancy** (daily 10am–5pm; charge; www.animalorphanagekenya.org) which has successfully bred the mountain bongo, an endangered large antelope that has effectively been an endemic Kenyan montane forest subspecies since it was extirpated in Uganda a century ago.

Samburu-Buffalo Springs and Shaba Reserves

The contiguous **Samburu-Buffalo Springs National Reserves** ❼ are the northernmost of the popular game parks. At 300 sq km (116 sq miles), the area is small by Kenyan standards. Its attraction lies in the beauty of the landscape and the concentration of wildlife, including several species not found outside this region. Shaba National Reserve is 9km (5.5 miles) to the east of Buffalo Springs on the other side of the road.

The reserves are roughly a two-hour drive north of Nanyuki. The tarmac ends at Isiolo, a service town with a mixed community of native Borans and Somali Muslims. There is a police

Mountain Sickness

More people die of pulmonary oedema on Mount Kenya each year than on any other mountain. It is caused by an accumulation of water on the lungs. The symptoms are headaches, nausea, sleeplessness, loss of appetite, swelling and fluid retention, breathing difficulties, slurred speech and abnormal behaviour. The only cure is to get to a lower altitude – as quickly as possible. To avoid pulmonary oedema, allow time to get accustomed to the altitude before going higher up.

Samburu tribesman

checkpoint at the end of town, where you may be asked to stop – and, if you do, will need to fend off the harmless but assertive jewellery sellers who besiege the tourist vans.

Once past the checkpoint, the bumpy dirt road enters the land of the Samburu, a pastoral tribe related to the Maasai. Tall and slender, they resemble the Maasai in native dress and decorative jewellery, and the hair of the warriors is styled with ochre-coloured clay. Several villages consisting of low huts made of woven branches coated with mud and sisal mats lie on the outskirts of the reserves, and you will see many Samburu tending their herds of goats and cattle.

The Ewaso Ngiro River divides the two reserves, with Samburu on the north bank and Buffalo Springs on the south. No river in Kenya is free from crocodiles, and this one has its fair share of particularly large, impressive ones.

Samburu National Reserve receives a steady stream of visitors, and there are several upmarket lodges and luxury tented camps for accommodation. The wild, acacia-dotted landscape surrounds Koitogor Mountain in the middle of the reserve, while the red granite outcrop of Ololokwe rises outside the northern boundary.

Buffalo Springs is named after the underground springs here, which attract a steady stream of thirsty wildlife in the dry season. The natural pool created by this event is one of the few places in the reserve where you can get out of your vehicle and swim safely, making it a popular picnic spot, with superb views across the marsh to the Wamba Mountains.

Shaba National Reserve was established at the same time as Samburu and Buffalo Springs. The northern area stretches 34km (21 miles) along the Ewaso Ngiro River with a number of springs and swampy areas. The rugged Shaba Hill dominates the southern part of the reserve. The well-appointed Sarova Shaba Lodge is an oasis in the bush with a natural spring cascading through the main buildings, and Joy's Camp, situated at Joy Adamson's original campsite, also overlooks a spring.

Animals migrate freely between the three reserves, as do the guests on their daily game drives. Of special interest is the Grevy's zebra, which is larger than the common zebra, with thin stripes, trumpet-shaped ears and a white belly. Its range is restricted to northern Kenya and a small part of southern Ethiopia, as is that of the reticulated giraffe, which roams the area in large numbers. The highly distinctive bronze, web-patterned coat and white markings of the reticulated giraffe make it the most handsome of the three varieties (see page 39). Other rare species endemic to this area include the Beisa oryx, the blue-legged Somali ostrich and the gerenuk, also known as the 'giraffe gazelle' because of its long neck, slender frame and its habit of standing on its hind legs to nibble at tree branches.

Green Crater Lake, Naivasha

THE GREAT RIFT VALLEY

The **Great Rift Valley** is part of a geological fault that runs across Africa from the Zambezi Delta in Mozambique to the Jordan Valley. It was formed in the Pleistocene era, when the collision of two parallel plates thrust the harder rock upwards, while the softer rock dropped nearly 1,000m (around 3,280ft) to form a wide trench bottom. The resulting chain of lakes and extinct volcanic cones that run along the Rift Valley, as it cuts through the highlands and descends into the Maasai Plains, makes it Kenya's most distinguishing topographical feature.

Many safari holidays feature a visit to one or two of the Rift Valley lakes, which stretch out along a north–south axis from Lake Turkana in the far north to Lake Magadi, which is completely dry and the source of the world's largest soda deposits. Those with a special interest in birdwatching should plan to spend a little more time in this area, as an extraordinary number of resident and migratory species congregate around the central lakes.

The lakes lie in the valley floor, surrounded by a fairly tame landscape of farmland in the south and overgrazed scrubland further north. There are several good viewpoints overlooking the Rift Valley – particularly the one facing the dormant volcano, Mount Longonot – along the eastern escarpment on the main road north from Nairobi. The most dramatic landscape, seemingly more characteristic of the Rift Valley's turbulent past, is along the C51 highway between Marigat and Eldoret. It climbs through the pretty sculpted shapes of the Tugen Hills to Kabarnet before dropping down sharply through the Kerio Valley and back up again along the high, twisted roads and spectacular vistas of the Elgeyo Escarpment. At Iten the scenery and road conditions change abruptly as you cross a high plateau to Eldoret.

Lake Naivasha

The closest lake to Nairobi, **Lake Naivasha** ❽ is as much a weekend retreat for city residents as a stop-over for tourists. At 1,890m (6,201ft) it is the highest of the Rift Valley lakes. The reed-rimmed shoreline, with its floating clumps of papyrus, changes constantly with the fluctuating water level. You can fish for black bass and tilapia, but the main attraction of this freshwater lake is

Lewa Wildlife Conservancy, Laikipia Plateau

its birdlife, which is best observed on a boat trip to the wildlife sanctuary on Crescent Island. The island is actually the outer rim of a volcanic crater that forms the deepest part of the lake. Here, as at all of Kenya's lakes, take extra precautions against mosquitoes from dusk to dawn. The mighty, yellow-barked acacias around the lake were called 'fever trees' by the early settlers who thought they were somehow responsible for malaria. In fact, both the trees and mosquito larvae thrive near large bodies of water.

Formerly Maasai country, the irrigated agricultural land around the lake is still largely owned by Europeans. It is used to grow vegetables and flowers, mainly for export.

Flamingo facts

Two species of flamingo live in Africa. These are the Greater Flamingo – taller and white – and the Lesser Flamingo, which is much pinker in overall colour, and greatly outnumbers its larger cousin. The pink hue of the flamingo's white features is caused by a carotene pigment in the algae.

Hell's Gate National Park

A few kilometres down South Lake Road is **Hell's Gate National Park ❾**. Though small in area – 68 sq km (26 sq miles) – the landscape is impressive, with some spectacular rock formations and steep, fiery basalt cliffs enclosing vast stretches of open grassland. This is one of the few savannah reserves where you can leave your vehicle and explore on foot. The volcanic pinnacle called Fischer's Tower, named after an early German explorer, marks the entrance to the gorge. There is a warden's post and information centre about 11km (7 miles) in from the Elsa Gate, where a nature trail leads to Ol Basta, a second volcanic plug. The clouds of steam emitted from the adjacent ridgetop mark the Olkaria Geothermal Station.

A pair of rare lammergeyers was once numbered among the many raptors nesting in the cliffs, but recent attempts to re-establish this handsome vulture have not met with lasting success. There is plenty of wildlife though: giraffe, impala, hartebeest, zebra and Grant's and Thomson's gazelle all graze in the grasslands among the whistling acacia thorn bushes, along with buffalo and the majestic eland.

Lake Nakuru

Lake Nakuru is famous for the multitude of flamingos that flock here to feed on the algae. The lake has no outlet and so minerals build up, giving the water a high alkaline content. Algae thrive on it, and so in turn do the flamingos.

At times, up to two million birds amass here, forming a pink ribbon around the entire perimeter of the lake, best viewed from the picnic site at the top of the Baboon Cliffs. At other times, especially when exceptionally heavy rainfall causes the water level to rise and a corresponding decrease in alkalinity, the flamingos disperse to other lakes in the Rift Valley, primarily Bogoria. Nevertheless, many thousands of flamingo can usually be seen, alongside the plentiful pelicans that fish here for tilapia.

Lake Nakuru National Park ❿ surrounds the lake, a mixed landscape of acacia woodland and rocky cliffs. It provides a habitat for over 450 species of bird, as well as lion, leopard, Rothschild's giraffe and waterbuck among others. Hippo Point, complete with a resident group of hippos, can be difficult to drive near to, as the land around it is muddy and unstable. Black and white rhino, translocated from other parts of the country, have bred successfully to restock other national parks, and are easily seen. To protect them from poachers, an electric fence has been erected around the park's entire perimeter.

Lesser flamingos at Lake Nakuru

National reserve

Lake Bogoria is the best place in Kenya to see the greater kudu, the local population of which was nearly wiped out by rinderpest disease in the 1890s. The second largest antelope, with white stripes and long, spiral horns, the greater kudu is common further south in Africa, but very rare in Kenya. In 1973, a 107 sq-km (41 sq-mile) area around the Lake Bogoria was designated a national reserve, largely for its protection.

Immediately east of the national park, the newly opened **Soysambu Conservancy** ⓫ (www.soysambuconservancy.org) is a 198 sq km (78 sq mile) private conservancy centred upon Lake Elmentaita, set below a striking volcanic plug whose outline does indeed evoke the Sleeping Warrior referred to in its Maasai name Elngirigata Ol Morani. Smaller than Nakuru or Naivasha, and set entirely within private land, Elmentaita is another alkaline lake that periodically hosts large flocks of flamingos and is reliably dense with other aquatic birds. Since 2010, one large lodge and three more intimate tented camps have opened in the conservancy, which protects a similar selection of species to Lake Nakuru National Park (but no rhino or lion) and can also easily be used as a base to visit it.

Lake Bogoria

After the drive through the sun-baked landscape broken only by goats scavenging along the roadside and termite mounds rising like sandcastles between the bushes, the eponymous waters of **Lake Bogoria National Reserve** ⓬, lying to the south of Lake Baringo, may seem like a mirage. Early explorers who discovered it on their expeditions to Uganda described it as the most beautiful view in Africa, and, indeed, the sight of Bogoria's steaming geysers set against the backdrop of the lake's rocky precipices is quite magnificent.

A local legend claims that the lake was formed when the god Chebet, angered by the meanness of the Kamale tribe towards passing travellers, invoked a deluge that lasted for days and wiped out their village. Lake Bogoria, now protected in a national reserve, is still called 'the place of the lost tribe'.

Although the steaming springs may well look like the fury of the gods, they are actually the remnants of past volcanic activity. You can get out of your car for a closer look at the sulphurous pools, which bubble like a cauldron. Brave picnickers have been known to boil their

Lake Bogoria National Reserve

eggs in the water. However, great care should be taken when walking near the springs, as the earth's crust is very thin, with scalding water simmering just below the surface. This area is very remote, and it's a long way to the nearest burns unit.

Like Lake Nakuru, Bogoria's waters are alkaline, and if you haven't seen many flamingos at Nakuru, you'll probably find them here. And when flamingos aren't present in any great numbers, more than 350 other bird species have also been recorded here.

Birdwatching tours and special game drives to seek the rare greater kudu can be arranged at the Lake Bogoria Hotel, which you will find just outside the Loboi Gate. In addition, there are three campsites on the southern side of the lake.

An African darter at Lake Baringo

Lake Baringo

The northernmost of the central Rift Valley lakes, **Baringo** ⑬ is a freshwater lake with abundant stocks of tilapia and catfish. The cloudy, brown colour of the water comes from the deposits of topsoil washed down during the rains; this erosion also accounts for its shallowness – over its entire 168 sq km (65 sq miles) it is no deeper than 12m (39ft).

Hippos wallow throughout the lake and graze on its shore at night, often wandering on to the lawns of the Lake Baringo Club, the only lodge on the lakeshore. Crocodiles are also numerous, but do not reach any great size here.

With some 470 species recorded around the lake, the area is a bird-lover's paradise. One of the islands hosts a large nesting colony of goliath herons, the tallest herons at 1.5m (5ft). The cliff-nesting Verreaux's eagle, water-loving great white egrets, and a variety of hornbills are also draws. A stay at one of the lake's two island camps includes watersport activities, hiking, birdwatching and fabulous views over the lake to the edges of the Rift Valley.

Hour-long boat trips out on the lake are available through the lodges or private operators. You'll see magnificent fish eagles, hippos and other wildlife on the shores of the islands.

You can make another excursion to a traditional village inhabited by the local Njemps, relatives of the Maasai whose lifestyle revolves around fishing rather than rearing livestock.

WESTERN KENYA

Western Kenya is not a common destination on the tourist trail. But for the return visitor to Kenya, or maybe for those who have the time and the interest to look beyond the game parks and beach resorts, it offers an amazing diversity of environments, from swampland and mountain wilderness to equatorial rainforest and the sultry shores of Lake Victoria.

Much of western Kenya is heavily populated, with fertile farmland and several small, busy market towns. The bulk of Kenya's tea plantations and sugar cane fields are found in this region. The Luo are the largest ethnic group, occupying the lowlands along the lakeshore, followed by the Luyha in the area north of Kisumu, the Nandi around Eldoret, the Kipsigis in the Kericho district and the Gush in the Kisii hills.

Dusty, noisy **Eldoret** is one of the fastest growing towns in Kenya. There is little to do or see here, but the tourist class hotels, banks and post office make it an adequate stop-over en route to more interesting places in the area.

Saiwa Swamp National Park

Kenya's smallest national park, **Saiwa Swamp ⑭**, is worth a visit to admire the unique ecological habitat confined within its 200ha (500 acres). The park was created in 1984 to protect the sitatunga (pronounced 'statunga'), a semi-aquatic antelope that is only found in this habitat. This small, reddish-brown creature spends most of the day submerged in the water with only the tip of its nose sticking out. It emerges to feed in the early morning and late afternoon, dipping down again at the slightest inkling of danger. You can spy on it from the cover of a tree-hide overlooking the swamp .

The boggy terrain is caused by the run-off from Mount Elgon. You can easily explore the trails in two to three hours and in normal footwear, as walkways and bridges have been built over the swamp. It is a delightful walk through indigenous rainforest. Vervet, colobus and the very localised white-bearded DeBrazza's monkey crash through the high branches overhead. From the five observation towers, you can look out over the swamp and catch sight of the many bird species, which number over 300, and include gems such as the beautiful double-toothed barbet and Ross's turaco.

Mount Elgon National Park

Mount Elgon ⑮ has been called 'Kenya's loneliest park', and this extinct volcano straddling the Ugandan border is indeed remote. Lower than Mount Kenya, but with a much larger base, it has similar vegetation and wildlife. The southeastern slopes of the mountain actually fall within the boundaries of Mount Elgon National Park. During the rainy months, the roads are impassable and the upper slopes are hidden in the clouds, making December to March the best time to visit. For those prepared to make the journey, the rewards are great: impressive cliffs, hot springs, mountain streams, massive trees and dense forest provide some of the best hiking in the whole of Kenya. A climb to Koitoboss Peak and the hot springs at Suam Gorge (which lie in Uganda) is also possible.

Of greatest interest to most visitors are the elephant caves – the most famous of which is Kitum – on the lower slopes inside the park. These huge caves extend horizontally into the mountain and are thought to have been carved out by elephant tusks. Amazingly, the giant pachyderms make their way up the rocky forest slopes to gouge lumps of sodium from this massive, natural salt lick. You can see the tusk marks on the cave walls. If you arrive early in the morning, you may still be able to catch some animals at the salt licks before they retreat into the forest. When walking up to the caves, keep an eye out for buffalo or giant forest hogs; take care also when entering the caves themselves. Should you wish to explore the depths of the

caves, you will need a strong torch. Note, too, that there are scores of (harmless) fruit bats hanging from the roof.

Because of Mount Elgon's remote position on the Ugandan border, there were once security problems associated with armed rebels and elephant poachers. Things have calmed down in recent years, but you might still ask around before setting off up the mountain. You should be safe enough in the park itself, as rangers at the gate will be able to offer advice and an escort if necessary.

Kakamega Forest National Reserve

Birdwatcher in Kakamega Forest National Reserve

Situated to the north of Kisumu, **Kakamega Forest National Reserve** is Kenya's only remaining equatorial rainforest. Once part of a vast, continental tract that stretched to the Atlantic Ocean, the 238 sq-km (92 sq-mile) reserve now attracts both nature experts and scientists as well as tourists to explore this isolated environment, one which no longer exists elsewhere in East Africa. A local guide can help you make the most of your visit by explaining the forest ecosystem and identifying some of the unique trees and plants found here, as well as the resident wildlife. Colourful butterflies and around 330 different bird species are resident in the forest, including several dozen that occur nowhere else in Kenya, among them the charismatic great blue turaco.

Fishing boats on Lake Victoria

Kisumu and Lake Victoria

The broad, clean streets and white buildings of **Kisumu** ⑰ are a pleasant surprise for the travel-weary. In this languid, lakeside town you can go about your business without too many hassles from the beggars and souvenir sellers you encounter elsewhere. Either it's just too hot to bother, or this inland port, which has long served as a crossroads for African, Asian and European traders, takes foreigners for granted.

In 1901 the railway line finally reached Port Florence, as the town was then called, completing a trade link with Uganda across the lake. Considerable heat, high levels of humidity, as well as outbreaks of sleeping sickness, malaria and blackwater fever made it the least desirable posting in the British Empire. However, by the start of World War II it had become a major East African transportation hub and administrative centre. Kenya's third-largest city fell into decline with the disbanding of the East African Community in 1977 and the drop in lake traffic. Today it has a mixed aura of charm and decay, and even an air of optimism as light industry replaces the rusting ships and empty warehouses along the shore.

The **Kisumu Museum** (daily 9.30am–6pm; charge; www. museums.or.ke) is a short walk or ride east of town. An incredible specimen of taxidermy stands, on its forelegs, in the main exhibition hall: a frantic wildebeest with an attacking lioness clinging to its back. Less dramatic, but equally interesting are the collections of musical instruments displayed here. (You will also see toys and other traditional artefacts of West Kenyan

ethnic groups.) The museum grounds contain a Luo homestead, a rather uninspiring aquarium, a turtle pond, crocodile
pit and a snake house that is brighter than the one in Nairobi.

In the town itself, Kisumu's market is delightful, the largest
in western Kenya and a good place to find a bargain. But the
real attraction is **Lake Victoria** ⓲, the second-largest freshwater
lake in the world. The main roads are set inland from the water's
edge, so you can't really stroll along the shore. Swimming is
absolutely out of the question, as bilharzia, a nasty parasite, is
present in the water. The best way to enjoy the lake is to take a
boat trip or ferry from the dock to one of the small islands, or
to stroll or drive out of town towards Hippo Point – site of the
lovely Kiboko Bay Resort, a great spot to enjoy the sunset over
the lake, occasionally accompanied by grunting hippos.

Kericho

Before or after your trip to Maasai Mara (see page 72), particularly if you've spent a long time on the hot, dry and dusty road,

Rusinga Island

Rusinga is the best known of Lake Victoria's small islands. A wealth of
prehistoric fossils have been found here, including Mary Leakey's discov-
ery of the skull *Proconsul africonus*, an early man-like ape. Rusinga was
also the birthplace of one of Kenya's greatest statesmen, Tom Mboya. A
Luo politician beloved by many Kenyans, he was assassinated by Kikuyu
gunmen in 1969 to the detriment of the whole country.

You can reach the island by ferry or overland via a new causeway.
Alternatively, take a flying safari, operated by Private Wilderness or Gov-
ernor's Camp in the Maasai Mara. You'll be flown from your nearest
airstrip for a half-day fishing trip or overnight excursion at the Rusinga
Island Lodge or Mfangano Island Camp. The boat trip across the lake is
great fun, even if you don't want to fish.

you may find yourself, for the first time in your life, crying out for rain. There's one place that guarantees satisfaction – **Kericho**  with its famous tea plantations about 250km (155 miles) northwest of Nairobi. Almost every day, at 3pm, dark clouds gather and burst into refreshing showers.

You can enjoy this spectacle from the comfort of your armchair at the **Tea Hotel**, where the unmistakable Englishness of the immaculate green lawns and flower gardens is a welcome change from the arid, red savannah. Built in 1952 as a clubhouse for the Brooke Bond tea company, to stay at the hotel is to take a delightful step back in time. The place is a swansong of the colonial era, and the rooms have their original 1950s-style furnishings, though if only one adjective were to be used to describe the hotel, it would more likely be 'rundown' than 'charming'.

The **tea plantations** are well worth a visit. There are kilometres of lush green bushes packed in a shoulder-high carpet

Tea plantation, Kericho

dotted with the heads of tea-pickers plucking the buds and topmost young leaves and tossing them into wicker baskets on their backs. With advance arrangements, you can also visit the tea factories on estates near the town for an explanation of the cutting, fermenting and drying stages in tea processing.

Kenya's tea industry prospered in the 1920s when experts decided that the soil here was perfect for producing the best-quality tea from Ceylonese and Indian plants. It is an example of how the British Empire functioned as a gigantic holding company, enabling the transfer of whole industries from one continent to another. Today, the Kericho plantations cover 15,000ha (37,000 acres), and the tea industry as a whole lies just behind tourism as Kenya's main foreign income earner.

Maasai Mara

If your trip to Kenya allows you time to visit only one game park, make it this one. The **Maasai Mara National Reserve** ❷⓿, an extension of Tanzania's Serengeti National Park, gives you the best chance of seeing all Africa's best known savannah dwellers in a superb rolling landscape of gentle hills and majestic acacia woodland.

This is one of the few places left in Africa where you can see animal herds roaming the plains in the vast numbers that early explorers once witnessed. Between the end of August and October, the fresh pasture of the Mara grasslands attracts up to 1.5 million wildebeest, accompanied by hundreds of thousands of zebras and gazelles, who migrate there from the Serengeti Plains in one of nature's grandest spectacle. Moving in groups of up to 20,000 at a time, the wildebeest thunder across the plains, hesitating for hours, sometimes days, at the edge of the Mara River, until the pressure of their numbers forces the leaders to plunge into the swirling waters. Many perish before reaching the opposite bank, drowning in the rushing river or victims of the waiting crocodiles.

The Mara has the largest population of lions in Kenya, and you'll have a good chance of spotting a leopard in the wild here. The waters of the Talek and Mara rivers are abundant with hippo and there are large herds of elephant and buffalo.

The Mara is Maasai country; Mara, in fact, is a Maasai word meaning 'spotted' or 'mottled', a reference to the acacia trees dotting the plains. The 1,670- sq-km (645-sq-mile) area is a national reserve, and Maasai herdsmen are permitted to reside with their cattle on parts of the land.

While you do have the opportunity here to seek out the more elusive game, you must be careful not to drive too close or disturb the animals and their prey. It is advisable to have a four-wheel drive vehicle and to enrol the help of a guide who knows the area.

The Maasai

The Maasai is Kenya's most famous tribe. Eighteenth century migrants from the Sudanese or Ethiopian Nile Valley, these proud, nomadic people soon came to control the fertile grasslands of the Rift Valley and the plains from Lake Turkana to Kilimanjaro. A pastoral people, they traditionally herd cattle, moving regularly in search of water and fresh pasture, and have a reputation for resisting the encroachment of modern life.

Several related families live together in low, circular huts (manyattas) constructed by the women out of mud mixed with cow dung. Their diet consists of milk, maize and blood extracted from their cattle, which they rarely use for meat. The size of a Maasai's herd is a symbol of his wealth. The Maasai believe that God gave them all the cows in the world; the other animals belong to God and must not be harmed; only eland and buffalo, the 'wild cattle', can occasionally be hunted for food.

The Maasai are polygamous and practise the circumcision and initiation rites that take a male from boyhood to warrior status. Despite conflict with the authorities, the proud, young morani, who carry clubs, swords and spears, still see the killing of a lion as a test of manhood.

The recently established **Mara Conservancy** manages the western part of the reserve, the Mara Triangle. This has brought together conservation professionals and the local Maasai communities, clamped down on poaching and restored roads and buildings. There are separate fees and guidelines for the Conservancy.

The remoteness of Maasai Mara adds to its adventure. Flying is the most convenient way to get there, and there are several small airstrips serving the lodges with daily flights from Nairobi. Though the 260-km (160-mile) drive across the Rift Valley from Nairobi is scenic in parts, the roads into

A male lion at Maasai Mara National Reserve

the park from Narok or Kericho are atrocious after heavy rain, so be prepared to push. The main tarmac road to Narok and beyond is also in bad condition. Accommodation is plentiful, with lodges, permanent tented camps and a number of campsites.

THE SOUTHEAST

Two of the country's best-known parks are located in this area: Amboseli, famed for its elephant herds, which can be seen against a photographic backdrop of a snow-capped Kilimanjaro; and the vast Tsavo, the country's largest national park, split into East and West.

Amboseli National Park

Zebra at Maasai Mara
National Reserve

Amboseli National Park ㉑ is relatively small and can easily be covered in a day – hence it receives heavy tourist traffic: short-term visitors dashing down from Nairobi and safari vehicles trekking through to nearby Tsavo. On the positive side, hordes of roving tourists make a poacher's job difficult, and, as a result, Amboseli is Kenya's foremost elephant park, with some of the country's finest mature tuskers. The sight of a herd of 40 or more of these creatures with the mellow evening sun setting over **Mount Kilimanjaro** (see page 13) is truly impressive.

Amboseli's environment is a precarious one. Its swamps provided the Maasai with a natural watering hole until the land was declared a national park in 1973. By then the combination of overgrazing and increased tourism had turned vast areas into near desert, and a sudden rise in the water table brought toxic salts to the surface, killing many trees. Extensive damage has also been caused by too much off-road driving. It's unlikely that this popular park will ever get the breathing space it needs to fully recover. Amboseli serves as a reminder of the fragility of a seemingly rugged landscape.

Tsavo National Park

Tsavo is the largest national park in Kenya. Its territory of 20,800 sq km (8,030 sq miles) has been split into two separately controlled parks, divided by the Nairobi–Mombasa highway. Vast elephant herds once roamed the plains of Tsavo, along with the largest population of black rhino in Africa, numbering in the high thousands. In the 1980s and early 1990s, over three-quarters of the elephants and nearly all of the rhino were wiped out by ruthless commercial poaching, but numbers have recovered to some extent since then, thanks to government's anti-poaching forces, which were strongly focused on Tsavo in the late 1990s.

The Ngulia Rhino Sanctuary in Tsavo West shelters most of the park's remaining rhino, which are making a gradual but steady recovery, and are also sometimes seen in the remote wilds of Tsavo East. The rest of the Big Five are well represented, and these, along with the wealth of other wildlife from the ubiquitous Marabou stork to the rare lesser kudu, account for Tsavo's popularity as a game-viewing mecca.

Tsavo West

Tsavo West ㉒ has the most spectacular landscape, an undulating plain peppered with green hills and rounded buttes

Young African elephants in Amboseli National Park

which are a legacy from the area's recent geological past. The nearby Chyulu Hills were created by volcanic action less than 500 years ago, and the Shetani Lava Flow on their southern edge is only 200 to 300 years old. There are trails leading across the lava rock to the top of the hill and into the Shetani Cave – bring a torch and walk with care. You can also scramble up the brittle, black slope to the rim of the Chaimu Crater, formed by another lava fountain. Always be alert for wild animals when exploring any of Tsavo's volcanic ruins.

The park's star attraction is the lush oasis of **Mzima Springs**. Rain falling in the Chyulu Hills is purified as it soaks through porous volcanic ash, and runs underground for 50km (31 miles) to resurface in two crystal-clear pools at Mzima.

Marabou Stork

Walk along the path through the palm trees and reeds lining the banks of the pools, home to crocodiles and hippos, and stop at the viewing tank submerged in the upper pool for a fish-eye's view of barbels and mud suckers. Vervet and Sykes monkeys dot the fig trees.

Three rivers – the Galana, Athi and Tsavo – flow through the park, attracting large concentrations of game. But the denser growth of vegetation after a period of rain can make it very difficult to see the animals. Rain also brings out that scourge of Tsavo, the tsetse fly. This variety does not carry sleeping sickness, like those in the Congo, but it has a nasty sting and will sometimes swarm in the open windows and roofs of safari vehicles when driving through a thicket. A blast of insect spray is the best way to rid your vehicle of these invaders (who are also said to be attracted to the colour blue).

Voi River outside Tsavo East National Park

The park has two lodges – Kilaguni Serena Safari Lodge (see page 140) and Ngulia Safari Lodge – and a number of luxury tented camps including Finch Hatton's (see page 139), Severin Safari Camp and Ngulia Safari Camp. The park is on a bird migration corridor, and ornithologists gather here to study the migration patterns of the many species. Both lodges have waterholes to attract wildlife.

Tsavo East

Tsavo East ㉓, the larger of the two parks, is flatter, drier and less frequently visited. Voi Safari Lodge (see page 140) is built into the side of a hill with a fantastic vista across the sweeping plain. It, too, has a floodlit waterhole with a photography hide alongside. There are a number of small tented camps, including Satao Camp (see page 140) in the southern part of the park, Satao Rock Camp just outside on the border, and Galdessa (see page 140) on the banks of the Galana River.

A distinguishing feature of Tsavo East is the stunning backdrop of the **Yatta Plateau**, one of the longest lava flows in the world. On the southern side of the plateau, the Tsavo and Athi Rivers join to form the Galana River just above Lugard's Falls, a series of rapids in a deep gorge cut into the bedrock by thousands of years of flowing water. Mudanda Rock is a popular haunt for the leopard and makes for excellent photo opportunities, as does Aruba Dam, which attracts abundant game in the dry season. There are numerous security patrols throughout the park.

THE COAST

This section covers Kenya's coast, including the island city of Mombasa, the beautiful beaches to the north and south, a series of spectacular offshore coral reefs, and characterful old Swahili ports such as Malindi and the UNESCO-protected island of Lamu.

Mombasa

The island-bound city of **Mombasa** ㉔, possibly Kenya's oldest town, was the medieval trade crossroads of Africa and Arabia. Its status as a port and trading centre is no less important now that tea and tourism have replaced gold and ivory as chief commodities.

The Man-Eaters of Tsavo

In 1898, during the construction of the railway, from Mombasa to Uganda a pair of elderly male lions on the Tsavo plains developed a taste for the workforce, eating at least 28 Indians and possibly more than 100 Africans. Somehow, the animals avoided every trap laid for them, and after a while one was even confident enough to board the train and drag off a victim. The terror lasted 10 months until the man-eaters were ambushed and shot. Thereafter, the country on both sides of the track was left as a wildlife reserve, later to become Tsavo East and West National Parks. The lions in this area retain a certain notoriety, but are less visually impressive than folklore suggests, since the males lack the imposing mane associated with lions elsewhere in Kenya.

Mombasa's origins may stretch back to 500BC, when Phoenician sailors put in at a coastal port that would correspond to Mombasa Island. The Greeks noted its trading potential in the 1st century AD, and later dhows, carried by the northeast monsoon from the Persian Gulf across the Indian Ocean, sailed along East Africa's coastal reef and found a navigable opening here. Over the ensuing centuries, it has been a magnet for Arabs, Persians, Turks, Indians and more recently the Portuguese and British, all of whom left their mark.

Kikois for sale, Diani Beach

In the 7th century, enterprising merchants from Persia and Arabia began to settle in the 'Land of the Zanj' (Land of Black People), bringing with them the Islamic faith. Over the next 300 years, the intermingling of races and religions produced the Arab-tinged Swahili language and Islamic coastal culture.

Mombasa basked in wealth and power until the end of the 15th century, when the Portuguese arrived to plunder the coast. It took nearly 100 years of repeated assaults before the island stronghold fell, but that century of siege destroyed medieval Mombasa. The town you see today is essentially 19th century, except for the remains of Fort Jesus, built by the Portuguese for their garrison in 1593. They in turn were driven out in 1730, and a period of unrest followed in which

The elephant tusks, Moi Avenue, Mombasa

Mombasa was ruled by the feuding Omani families who had aided the rebellion against the Portuguese. In the late 19th century, as a British protectorate, the town flourished once again.

Sightseeing in Mombasa can be covered in a day and is best done as early in the morning as possible, before your enthusiasm sinks into the torpor of the midday heat. The one monument you won't miss is the double arch across Moi Avenue formed by four huge, white, sheet metal tusks, erected in 1952 to commemorate the visit of Queen Elizabeth Ⓐ. The tourist information office sits just beyond the 'elephant' tusks.

Fort Jesus Ⓑ (daily 8am–6pm; charge; www.museums. or.ke), on the edge of the Old Town, is a good place to begin. Inscribed as a UNESCO World Heritage Site in 2011, it is strategically placed at the southern entrance to Mombasa harbour, set on a coral ridge and protected by ramparts several metres thick. The grounds include a barracks, chapel, water cistern and well, guard rooms, gunpowder storeroom and an Omani house filled with artefacts from the Arab period.

The Old Town, just north of Fort Jesus, is the most fascinating part of Mombasa. Along the main thoroughfare of Ndia Kuu Road you can see some of the city's finest Arab buildings with carved doors and delicate wooden balconies. The narrow streets contain many of Mombasa's 49 mosques, the oldest of which, on Bachawy Road, is the Mandhry, built in 1570.

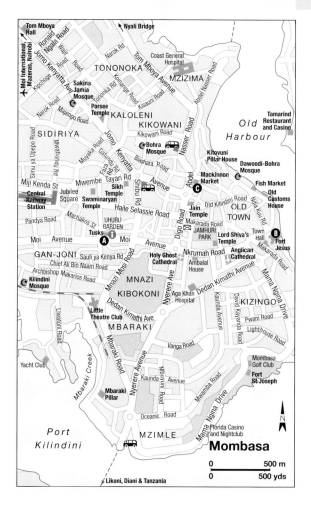

Mombasa

0   500 m
0   500 yds

Lovely Hindu temples can also be found throughout the city. Among the most striking are the **Swaminarayan Temple** on Haile Selassie Avenue, the **Jain Temple** off Digo Road, and the **Lord Shiva Temple** on the edge of the old town.

Gone are the days when tourists were welcomed aboard to join the haggling at the old dhow harbour. If you are lucky, you can watch the loading or unloading of the last of the dhows that still ply between Mombasa and the Gulf, their large lateen sails now supplemented by a motor.

A glut of curio shops line the alleys near the Fort Jesus car park, though many are overpriced. A more authentic atmosphere for browsing can be found at the **Municipal Market** ⓒ, still known by its colonial name, Mackinnon's Market. The adjacent Biashara Street is an excellent place to browse and shop for bright-coloured kangas and fabrics.

The South Coast

The Likoni Ferry links Mombasa to the south coast. Here you'll find that idyllic palm-fringed beach with soft, white sand of your dreams. Protected by a coral reef, the water offshore is warm and clear; surprisingly, the beaches here are quieter than most of the north coast's resort areas.

The best of the beaches is **Diani** ㉕, the major landmark of which is a 500-year-old baobab tree measuring 21m (71ft) in circumference, protected by presidential decree. Once you have seen the baobab, there is blissfully little to do but watch the sun rise and set, an often spectacular event.

There are plenty of watersports on offer all along the coast. Highly recommended is an excursion to **Wasini Island** and **Kisite-Mpunguti Marine National Park** ㉖. You will be collected from your hotel early in the morning for the hour's drive south to Shimoni, where a converted dhow takes you past coral islands to Kisite. The reef here offers some of the best snorkelling on the coast, but you can also gasp at the amazing corals and tropical fish by looking through glass-bottomed viewers from a small boat.

Following a gigantic lunch at **Charlie Claw's** (see page 108), or one of the other seafood restaurants on Wasini Island, you are entirely free to relax in the gardens or explore the island's early 19th-century Muslim village. On its edge are the stunning coral gardens. These surreal, honeycombed sculptures, spread over nearly 1ha (some 2.5 acres), were chiselled out by the fluctuating tides over the past 200 years. They remain, naturally, a work in progress.

Carpenter at work in the Old Town

If you want to give your suntan a rest, go inland to **Shimba Hills National Reserve** ㉗. The pleasant, wooded plateau rises to 450m (1,475ft), giving a refreshing change from the oppressive heat of the coast. Go early in the morning for the best chance to see the reserve's best known residents, Kenya's only population of the splendid sable antelopes. Noted for their scimitar-shaped horns, the male sable has a magnificent reddish-black coat, while the females are a lovely chestnut-brown colour. Other wildlife includes buffalo and elephant, though the latter are more easily observed in the neighbouring **Mwaluganje Sanctuary** (www.elephantmwaluganje.com), an admirable community

Birdwatching at Shimba Lodge, Shimba Hills National Reserve

ecotourism project whose baobab- and cycad-studded hills slope down to a wildlife-rich waterhole in front of Mwaluganje Elephant Camp, the only accommodation within the sanctuary.

The North Coast

The north coast is where Mombasa's elite have their homes, palatial residences shrouded in hibiscus and bougainvillea. This stretch of the coast is peppered with luxury hotels too.

There are, however, several attractions to divert you from the sun and sea. **Mamba Village** (www.mambavillage.com) is the largest crocodile farm in Africa. You can walk along a shady pathway to observe some of its 10,000 reptiles basking in a series of breeding pools reclaimed from an old limestone quarry. Five o'clock is feeding time, when you can watch the crocs jump as high as 2m (6.5ft) out of the water for their dinner. There are also lovely botanical gardens, an aquarium with live corals, camel and horseback rides and a restaurant.

The Swiss agronomist Réné Haller was awarded a UN environmental protection prize for his success in converting the wasteland of a stone quarry into **Haller Park** (formerly Bamburi Nature Trail; daily 8am–5pm). This small forest harbours serval cats, monitor lizards, owls and other wildlife, including a pair of hippos in the central lake and giraffes.

North to Malindi

There are two sets of Arab ruins as you head north to Malindi. The first is at **Jumba la Mtwana** (Home of the Slave Master) outside Mtwapa, a 14th-century Swahili town whose ruined coral houses and mosques stretch down to the sea.

More substantial is the ancient town of **Gedi** ㉘ (daily 7am–6pm; charge; www.museums.or.ke), founded in the late 13th or early 14th century. The ruins here are extensive and well preserved; you can seek out the old mosques with their deep wells along eerie trails through the jungle, or pick your way among the walls of the palace, houses and pillar tombs. Rooms such as the 'House of the Scissors' and 'House of the Venetian Bead' indicate where Gedi's most interesting finds were made, many of which can be seen in the small museum. Next door to Gedi is the **Kipepeo Butterfly Farm** with a delightful Butterfly House.

Gedi lies close to the pretty small beach resort of **Watamu** ㉙, where the beautiful Turtle Bay is lined with quality resorts such as Hemingway's and Turtle Bay Beach Club (see page 141). The offshore coral gardens here rank among the best snorkelling sites in East Africa, and there is great diving in the vicinity, while Mida Creek is one of the top sites in the country for marine birds.

On the main Mombasa–Malindi road facing the turn-off to Gedi and Watamu, the **Arabuko-Sokoke National Park** ㉚ protects the country's largest remaining stand of coastal forest. There is a Visitors' Centre from where you can walk along a nature trail or explore deeper along a few 4x4-only access roads. This forest is home to several rare and endemic creatures, among them the bizarre golden-rumped elephant shrew (which is often seen at Gedi), and the Sokoke scops owl, Sokoke pipit and Clark's weaver.

Malindi

If you're looking for deep relaxation and just want to bask for a week or two in the sun, then **Malindi** ❸ may be the place for you. Visitors are well catered for in this old Swahili town, which now relies solely on tourism for its prosperity. There is some excellent fishing and a pleasant market to browse through for souvenirs. However, it's usually too hot to move around, so you don't have to feel guilty about relaxing by the pool until you fly home.

There was a time when Malindi was more lively. With an eye to the main chance, the Sheikh of Malindi welcomed Vasco da Gama on that 1498 journey, giving him provisions for his voyage to India. His hospitality paid off with some golden years of trade with Portugal during the 16th century, until the rival state of Mombasa was conquered and the Portuguese transferred the sheikh there. Malindi then sank back into the torpor you'll encounter today.

Marine park

Just outside Watamu is the Watamu Marine National Park. Like its neighbour, Malindi Marine National Park, it is a protected area of white, coral sand beaches and clear, deep-blue lagoons where it is forbidden to fish or collect coral and seashells. An afternoon sundowner dhow trip into Mida Creek offers a chance for birdwatching along the edges of the mangroves and mudflats. Trips in glass-bottomed boats out to the coral reefs will be available from any of the hotels at Watamu or Malindi.

There's a monument to that brief moment of glory, out along the cliffs on the promontory, at the southern end of the Malindi harbour. The brilliant white Vasco da Gama pillar, engraved with Portugal's coat of arms, was erected by the explorer in gratitude to the sheikh for his warm reception. It has survived the ravages of the Turks, Arabs and British and is one of the very few authentic Portuguese relics left on the coast.

Other sites of interest include a pair of 15th-century pillar tombs, of a type unique to the Swahili Coast, and the facing Malindi Tourist Market, which offers at least 50 craft stalls to curio hunters. On the waterfront, less than five minutes walk south, the Malindi Museum (daily 8am–6pm; charge; www.museums.or.ke) is housed in a colonnaded three-storey building that started life as an Indian trading centre in 1891. Nearby, the small Portuguese Chapel of St Francis Xavier, built around 1542, is East Africa's oldest church.

Vasco da Gama Pillar, Malindi

Lamu

For an idea of what Malindi or Mombasa looked like when the Arabs ruled the coast, make the trip to the island of **Lamu** ㉜, a backwater of Swahili culture off Kenya's northern shore. Its origins date to the 2nd century and along with Manda and Pate it was one of the most prosperous commercial centres of the archipelago until its decline in the late 1800s. Unlike its neighbours, Lamu survived, remaining isolated from modern technology and the Western world until shipping and the wave of tourism brought a resurgence to its economy in the 1960s.

It is best reached by small aircraft on one of the regular, inexpensive flights from Nairobi, Malindi or Mombasa, as the overland route is rough and often flooded. You'll be welcomed at the airstrip on Manda Island by an eager gang of locals ready to carry

An ornate door in Lamu

your bags to the ferry for the short crossing to Lamu.

Your first few hours in Lamu may prove something of a cultural shock. There are no cars here; the main mode of transport is donkeys and they and their droppings are everywhere. Open sewers run alongside the narrow streets, and refuse is often dumped into the sea. But you soon forget the unsanitary sights and smells as you fall into the languid rhythm of this town.

The traditional Islamic community has made few concessions to the modern world. Women, especially, should be dressed in a conservative manner to avoid causing offence, though you'll feel pretty conspicuous in shorts when everyone else is swathed in black from head to toe. Be extra sensitive about photographs here; always ask before you point your camera at someone.

Lamu's stone houses are the best legacy of Swahili architecture. These plain, thick, coral walls often conceal elaborate interior ornamentation of carved plasterwork and wall niches. You can see a fine example, restored to portray the early way of life, at the **Swahili House Museum**.

The most beautiful feature of Lamu's houses is their carved wooden doors. Some date to the 18th century, but even the most modern retain the style, forms and craftsmanship of centuries-old traditions. There are excellent specimens on display at the **Lamu Museum** (daily 9am–6pm; charge includes entrance to the town's other historical monuments; www.museums.or.ke). One of the finest small museums in Kenya, it offers explanations of Lamu's architecture and insights into the traditions of this complex culture. The pride of the museum are two magnificent *siwas* (ceremonial horns), one of carved ivory 2m (6.5ft) long and the other, slightly shorter, of brass.

You can eat seafood for a song at the small restaurants along the waterfront, but only a few places sell alcohol. These include Petley's Inn, a landmark meeting place for locals and travellers alike, and the Peponi Hotel (see page 142), 3km (2 miles) down the road at Shela. This is Lamu's swimming beach, easily reached by dhow if you don't want to walk.

There are plenty of local boatmen to take you fishing or sailing on a dhow around the other islands. But the best way to spend your days in Lamu is to wander through its back streets, or simply sit on a rooftop or in the main square by the old fort, watching the world go by.

Sadly, in late 2011, the low-key tourist industry that thrives on Lamu's idyllic old world ambience was hit badly by two separate incidents wherein westerners were kidnapped and killed by Somali pirates. Both incidents occurred on isolated and unsecured beach locations, rather than in the town itself, but it may be some time before tourism resumes as normal.

Another threat to Lamu is the planned construction of a modern port to serve as the oceanic outlet of the mooted Lamu Port and Southern Sudan-Ethiopia Transport Corridor (LAPSSET) project, which would link Lamu to the rich oilfields of South Sudan. Sceptics fear that an influx of oil money might create a situation comparable to Nigeria's troubled Niger Delta, while the local community-based Lamu Environmental Preservation and Conservation (LEPAC) has voiced concerns about the impact on the environment and sensitive land ownership issues.

WHAT TO DO

SPORTS

Kenya offers wide opportunities for sports and outdoor recreation year-round due to its excellent climate. Watersports, hiking, fishing, climbing, tennis and riding are popular.

Watersports

Watersports of all types are prolific throughout Kenya. You will find the coastal waters delightfully warm for swimming, with none of the health risks or crocodiles of the inland rivers and lakes. The sharks stay outside the reef.

If you've never gone snorkelling before, Kenya's amazing coral reefs provide excellent opportunities. There are glass-bottomed boats that will take you out to the shallow reefs for hire at hotels and on the beaches; many of these boats have snorkelling gear on board. Wear rubber-soled shoes to protect your feet from the razor-sharp coral. Scuba-diving equipment can also be hired, and many hotels offer diving tuition.

Some beach resorts offer waterskiing, windsurfing and kite surfing. You can, in theory, waterski on some of the inland lakes (Lake Naivasha, Lake Baringo and Victoria), but the possibility of contracting bilharzia makes it a risky business; best

When to go

The best time of year to explore the marine world is October to March, when the northeast monsoon (*kaskazi*) blows. From April to September, the southeast kusi brings cooler conditions, rougher waters and high winds – though the water temperature never drops below 24°C (75°F).

Abseiling down Fisher's Tower, Hell's Gate National Park

Ballooning over the Maasai Mara National Reserve

to stick to the coast. Sailing is a great way to enjoy the inland waterways, the best spots being Lake Naivasha and Lake Victoria. If you're visiting Lamu, a dhow trip around the nearby islands is a timeless thrill. Canoeing and white-water rafting are also growing sports, and river trips can be arranged at some lodges and hotel resorts.

Deep-sea fishing can also be arranged on the spot through hotels along the coast. River and lake fishing can be booked through specialist travel agents.

Hiking and Climbing

Kenya's spectacular mountains and scenic hills make hiking a great lure. Some of the most accessible regions for walking include Mount Kenya, the Aberdare Mountains, the Chyulu Hills, Hell's Gate, and Mounts Susua and Longonot and the Menengai Crater in the Rift Valley. Ramblers in the Ngong Hills, southwest of Nairobi, should have a security guard. Further afield, Ololokwe Mountain just north of Samburu, the Cherangani Hills and Mount Elgon are considered superb walking country. Before setting off, pick up a good guidebook and detailed map of the region you plan to visit.

Experienced and fearless mountain climbers can attempt an ascent to the higher peaks of Mount Kenya. Climbs are organised by the Nairobi-based Mountain Club of Kenya or through your travel agent and begin at the Naro Moru River Lodge (see page 135), which hires out porters and equipment.

A reasonably fit novice can climb the lower peak, Lenana, in a couple of days.

Other Sports

Tennis and other racket sports are on offer at many of the larger hotels and sports clubs. Fitness centres and health spas can be found at a number of hotels and lodges around the country.

Riding is most popular in the Highlands. A good place to enquire about hiring horses is the Karen shopping centre outside Nairobi. Pony trekking and mountain biking through the Rift Valley or elsewhere can often be arranged through your lodge or hotel. Horse racing has been a popular sport in Kenya since the early 20th century, though the only racetrack to hold regular meetings is the Ngong Race Course on the outskirts of Nairobi. The season runs from September to July, when meetings are held most Sunday afternoons.

Golf is also popular, with hotels and country clubs across Kenya geared towards catering to the golfer's every whim.

Hot-Air Ballooning

Not for the light of pocket, nor for anyone adverse to extremely early mornings (a 5.30am start is typical), balloon safaris nonetheless offer a truly unique opportunity for game-spotting. They are particularly popular over the Maasai Mara, whose wide, open plains allow excellent visibility, and can be booked from the UK (through your tour operator) or on arrival in Kenya. You'll spend an hour or so drifting above the animals, before landing and being served a champagne breakfast out in the bush. Although these rides are expensive (around US$450), most people claim that they are money well spent. But for those whose budget doesn't quite stretch to it, even just watching the balloons drift over the plains at sunrise is impressive. One tip: take a hat to protect your head from the heat of the burner.

Bargain hunt

Bargaining is very much a part of life in East Africa. Seasoned shoppers advise that you start your bargaining at half the suggested price. If prices are marked, there is probably less room for negotiation.

SHOPPING

The big challenge in shopping for souvenirs of your stay in Kenya is sorting out genuine artworks from mass-produced junk. The first rule of thumb is to avoid any shop with a sign that offers 'curios'. These may well be hand carved on an assembly line, without the careful craftsmanship of the real thing.

Two good places in Nairobi to find authentic, quality African crafts are the Utamaduni Craft Centre, off Langata Road (www.utamaduni.com; a percentage is donated to wildlife conservation) and African Heritage (www.african heritage.net), with showrooms on the Mombasa Highway and at Carnivore Restaurant (see page 106). You can find cheaper goods at the city market, but you'll have to bargain hard. Craft co-operatives representing rural artisans have retail shops in the towns, and you can often visit textile, bead and woodcarving workshops on the outskirts. Visit the colourful open-air 'Maasai Markets' around Nairobi – at the Westgate Shopping Mall on Tuesdays, Junction Mall on Thursdays, Village Market on Fridays and at Yaya Centre on Sundays. If you can't make the major market days, the Triangle Market in Westlands is open seven days a week. For more quality souvenirs, visit the Banana Box (www.banana boxcrafts.com) at the Sarit Centre, Blue Rhino at ABC Place, and Collector's Den at the Hilton Hotel (www.collectors denkenya.com).

In Mombasa look out for antiques: Arab brasswork, trays and Zanzibar chests, although antique chests are harder to find now. The coast is also a good place to buy colourful fabrics – *kikois* for men, *kangas* and *kitenges* for women – which can be worn as beach wraps or used for bedspreads and tablecloths.

Note that animal skins or products bought without government permits – and you won't get one – are strictly illegal, as are game trophies and ivory products. Coral and seashells will probably have been plundered from one of the protected marine parks, so their purchase is also highly illegal.

ENTERTAINMENT

The big hotels in Nairobi, Mombasa and on the coast should be able to satisfy an urge for clubbing. You'll often be entertained by bands performing American and European pop music. Traditional African music can be difficult to track down. Native dancing is often performed at lodges and hotels,

Products for sale at the City Market, Nairobi

but it can bear the same relationship to the real thing as the curios in souvenir shops do to authentic African art.

A more genuine display of African dancing is available at the Bomas of Kenya, near Nairobi National Park, where you can see spectacular Samburu war dances, Kamba acrobatics, a Giriama wedding dance and an expurgated version of the Kikuyu circumcision ceremony that is still carried on by men though suppressed by women.

The publications *Going Out* (www.goingoutkenya.com) and *Go Places* (www.goplacesonline.com) list current exhibitions and cultural events in the capital. Nairobi's Gallery Watatu (www.gallerywatatu.com) and a number of art galleries in the upmarket shopping centres display contemporary African art.

Maasai dancing

CHILDREN

There are pros and cons of taking children on safari. There is lots to see, traditional accommodation offers a unique experience, and animal-loving children will be in their element. Babysitting is usually available in hotels and camps at a reasonable price. Most upmarket hotels and lodges have pools. However, most safaris involve long, bumpy journeys and some very early morning starts. Some safaris are not available to children under the age of 12 years.

Festivals and Events

Check www.kenyabuzz.com or the daily newspapers for weekly sporting, cultural and social event updates.

January Rhino Charge; www.rhinocharge.co.ke. Started in 1999, this annual bicycle fundraiser for Rhino Ark is an off-road event in which competitors must visit 13 points scattered over approximately 100 sq km within a 10 hour period.

February '10 to 4' Mountain Bike Challenge; www.mountkenyatrust. org. This one- or two-day downhill mountain bike race is another conservation fundraiser. It starts at the boundary of Mount Kenya National Reserve and finishes below the Laikipia Plains. Kijani Trust Music Festival; www.kijanikenyatrust.org. Classical and choral music are the main focus of this annual charity festival, which runs in two parts, one in Feb/March and the other in August.

March KCB Safari Rally; www.safarirally.net. Going back more than 50 years, this is regarded by many as the world's toughest motor rally, and is usually won by drivers based in Africa.

May Mombasa Marathon. This below-standard length marathon starts and ends in Mombasa Old Town, with low altitude compensating for the sticky climate. It has a long history of Kenyan winners male and female.

June Safaricom Lewa Marathon; www.lewa.org. Set in the Lewa Conservancy, this marathon (with a half-marathon option) is one of the few in the world where classic safari wildlife might be encountered.

August Maralal International Camel Derby. A host of camel related races and events take place at this fun weekend derby held in Maralal annually. Mombasa International Show; www.ask.co.ke. This premier agricultural show starts in late August, sometimes running into September.

October Malindi Fishing Festival. Reputedly the world's oldest angling festival, this is a must for serious game fisherman.

November Tusker Safari Rugby Sevens; www.safarisevens.kenyarfu. com. The Kenya leg of the world's premier rugby sevens competition. Lamu Cultural Festival, Kenya's most atmospheric old port is a fitting setting for this festival celebrating all aspects of Swahili and coastal culture.

EATING OUT

The variety of the cuisine in Kenya reflects the country's rich history. It was the Arabs who started the cosmopolitan trend in local cuisine here, sailing in with their dried fruits, rice and spices and expanding the diet of the coastal Swahilis. But it took centuries for this influence to spread inland, where people subsisted on a diet heavy in sorghum and millet, supplemented only by whatever fruits, roots and seeds they could find.

The arrival of the Portuguese in 1498 changed all that, with the introduction of foods from newly discovered Brazil. Maize, bananas, pineapples, chillies, peppers, sweet potatoes and manioc were all brought into East Africa, where most of them were destined to become local staples. The Portuguese

Vegetable shop, City Market, Nairobi

also brought lemons, limes and oranges from China and India, as well as introducing domestic pigs.

The British were next to influence eating and drinking habits in Kenya, importing new breeds of sheep, goats and cattle, together with luxuries such as strawberries and asparagus. They planted high-quality coffee and taught their cooks how

Cooking *chapati*

to make lumpy custard, as well as which way to serve the port with up-country 'Njoro Stilton'.

They also imported thousands of Indians to build the railway to Uganda, and with these immigrants came the curries, chapatis and chutneys that are now as traditional a Sunday lunch in Kenya as roast beef and Yorkshire pudding are in England. Later, between and after the wars, the Europeans arrived with their spicy sausages and pastas. More recently, global fast foods from hamburgers to pizzas have appeared in Nairobi.

In the 40 or so years since Kenya gained its independence from Britain the cuisine has been transformed by the influence of innumerable and varied cooking styles, from Ethiopian, Indian and Thai to French and Italian. The result is an incredible variety of high-quality food, usually at very reasonable prices.

Quantities are enormous and cheese and desserts are an honourable supplement to the meal, alongside the delicious, ripe pineapples, papayas and mangoes. On safari, you will be glad of the traditional English breakfasts usually served to satisfy appetites after a dawn game drive.

One of the great treats of Kenya is the wonderful fresh seafood served on the coast: large lobsters, superb shrimps and prawns, all astoundingly cheap compared with European or American prices – and excellent kingfish and swordfish. If you order them simply grilled, with at most a butter sauce, you will have tasted one of Kenya's best meals.

Vegetarians are well catered for at the hotels and lodges. In the cities and on the coast, there are many fine Indian, Italian and Chinese restaurants. Some excellent pizzas can also be found on the north coast in Malindi. African food can best be sampled at the African barbecues put on weekly by many hotels and lodges.

The buffet service, favoured by most hotels for at least one of their daily meals, gives you as generous a portion as you could wish. In Kenya, to eat well without spending a fortune, go for the buffet spreads and seafood.

Eating out is one of the great pleasures of Kenya. There are plenty of excellent restaurants in Nairobi and, at most of them, you'd be hard pressed to spend much more than £10 per person excluding wine, although at a few of the really expensive places you could pay three times as much, with appetisers and dessert. Still, wining and dining in Kenya won't cost the earth, even at the finer restaurants. You can eat well at most establishments at far less than European or American prices.

If you're after a quick snack, a number of Nairobi's shopping centres (Sarit, Yaya, ABC Place, Village Market, The Junction) have a selection of restaurants or food courts offering local dishes, salad bars, Italian, European, Indian and fast foods.

Outside Nairobi and the coast your choice of eating places is slim. Most safari camps and lodges include all meals in their rack rates, and elsewhere hotel restaurants are usually your best bet.

Local Cuisine

Traditionally, Kenyans breakfast on *mandazi* (a triangular-shaped doughnut) washed down with sweet milky tea. Lunch is *ugali* (corn meal porridge) eaten with vegetable or meat stew. Dinner might be *nyama choma* (grilled meat, often goat, sometimes chicken or beef) and the rural staple, *sukuma wiki*, which literally translates as 'getting through the week' and is a variation on spinach. *Irio*, a Kikuyu mixture of mashed potatoes and peas with maize kernels, is another dish to try, as is *kuku wakupaka*, a spiced chicken recipe from Lamu. Meat is typically accompanied by clay pots filled with sweet potatoes, arrowroot, cassava and other varieties of root vegetables.

Though the national cuisine may seem a little bland to visitors with adventurous culinary tastes, the wide and delicious range of other foods on offer more than makes up for

Spices for sale at MacKinnon Market, Mombasa

it. Fish-eaters can indulge in lobster, prawns, crayfish, Nile perch, tilapia (a freshwater fish similar to perch), parrot fish, or delicious smoked sailfish, the Kenyan equivalent to smoked salmon. Meat-eaters can eat their fill of zebra, gazelle, crocodile, giraffe, ostrich, or the rather more ordinary beef or Molo lamb.

Healthy-eating enthusiasts can tuck into passion fruit, paw-paw, guavas, pineapple, plums, oranges, bananas and other fruits. To see and sample the wide range of fresh vegetables and fruit on offer, you should call into Nairobi's City Market, where foods from asparagus to tree tomato will be for sale.

And don't miss snacks such as warm toasted cashew nuts, macadamia nuts and coconuts, or avocados with Worcestershire sauce. Other snacks to try include plantain, arrowroot or cassava chips.

Fish for sale in Kisumu

What to Drink

Kenya's local brews – Tusker Lager, White Cap and Pilsner – are excellent and inexpensive, served cool or warm according to your preference. In hotels and restaurants all imported wines and spirits are fairly costly. As far as wine is concerned, attempts were made to grow wine-producing grapes near Naivasha, but were abandoned when South African and European wines began to flood the market. Imported wine in restaurants is expensive by Kenyan standards, but not excessively so for European or American visitors. Wine in supermarkets is reasonably priced, considering how far it has travelled.

For liqueurs, locally grown options include the coffee-flavoured Kenya Gold or Kenya Cane, a white rum made from sugar cane and similar to Bacardi.

The Tamarind

Even if dining is all 'packaged' in your hotel holiday, try to escape for just one meal out at the superb Tamarind, of which there are branches in both Nairobi and Mombasa. In Nairobi, the Tamarind has sea-blue decor and consistently superb food, and a visit here is more an evening out than a meal: start in the upstairs bar with nibbles of tiny fried prawns, coconut strips and banana crisps. For a more substantial starter, try smoked trout with horseradish sauce, a mound of the minuscule Mombasa oysters, fish tartare or perhaps dried impala. For the main course, there are spiny lobsters, king crab claws, Malindi sole, or a mixture of the lot in a superb seafood casserole. Mombasa's Tamarind is Moorish-styled, set on a hill overlooking the city's old harbour, and has tables set out on the flower-filled terrace. The speciality of the house is also seafood: try lobster Tamarind, fish tartare, prawns piri piri and coupe bahari, or just order oysters and champagne and enjoy being alive. If you feel lucky, the Golden Key Casino is upstairs. Or, if you feel nautical, take the Tamarind Dhow and enjoy a romantic evening of seafood and light music while floating under the stars.

PLACES TO EAT

The majority of restaurants fall into the moderate range, hence we have not further classified them here; a two or three-course meal for two including local drinks will usually cost in the vicinity of US$30–40, more if you opt to drink wine (which is imported and typically costs US$20–30 per bottle). For details on average prices, refer to Budgeting For Your Trip, page 114.

NAIROBI

Abyssinia Exotic Ethiopian Restaurant *Brookside Grove, Westlands, tel: 073-361 5442, www.abyssiniarestaurantnairobi.com.* A great place to try Africa's most distinctive cuisine, a sourdough pancake-like staple called *injera* eaten with a variety of fiery 'wat' stews.

Carnivore *Langata Road, tel: 020-600 5933-7, www.tamarind.co.ke.* Very popular restaurant, where game and other meats are spit-roasted over charcoal and carved on to hot pewter plates at your table. A favourite of Kenyans and tourists alike.

China Plate *Chancery Building, Valley Road, tel: 020-271 9194.* Get past the uninspired location, on the first floor of a suburban office block, and the superb Szechwan cuisine and friendly service more than compensate.

Haandi Restaurant *The Mall, Westlands, tel: 020-444 8294/5/6, www.haandi-restaurants.com.* Popular, high-class Indian restaurant that does great food. You can watch the chefs through a glass wall. Reservations essential.

Karen Blixen Coffee Garden *336 Karen Road, tel: 073-361 6206, www.karenblixencoffeegarden.com.* Best known for its Sunday carvery, this outdoor restaurant also serves a good selection of continental-style sandwiches, snacks and full mains

Lord Delamere Terrace *Norfolk Hotel, Harry Thuku Road, tel: 020-221 6940.* Good lunches and light meals at this popular bar; the cuisine doesn't stray far from good, average international fare.

Mediterraneo Westlands *Woodvale Grove, Westlands, tel: 020-444 7494, www.mediterraneorestaurant.co.ke.* Popular Italian restaurant serving genuine homemade pasta and eclectic Italian dishes, with branches at the Junction Mall and in the suburb of Gigiri.

Nairobi Java House *ABC Place, Waiyaki Way, tel: 020-445 1978/9, www.nairobijavahouse.com.* This reliable local coffee house chain has a dozen branches citywide, serving good freshly-brewed coffee, along with a range of pastries, snacks and fast foods.

Pampa Churrascaria Grill *Panari Sky Centre, Mombasa Road, tel: 072-213 1047, www.pampagrillkenya.com.* Traditional south-Brazilian meat roasted in churrasco style, including a sumptuous buffet of hot and cold vegetables and salads. Brazilian wines also available.

Tamarind Nairobi *National Bank Building, Harambee Avenue, tel: 020-221811/220473, www.tamarind.co.ke.* This upcountry sister of its long-serving Mombasa namesake is arguably Nairobi's top seafood restaurant, but it's also good for steaks and other meat dishes.

Trattoria, Town House *Wabera/Kaunda Street, tel: 020-340855, www.trattoria.co.ke.* Centrally located and long-serving ristorante, pizzeria, posticceria, cafeteria and gelateria all in one. Open 8.30am–midnight.

Village Market Food Court *www.villagemarket-kenya.com.* Set in the eponymous shopping mall opposite the Tribe Hotel, this cosmopolitan cluster of fast food restaurants has everything from Indian and Thai to Lebanese and Kenyan, all at very reasonable prices, set around an open courtyard with ample seating.

CENTRAL HIGHLANDS

Barney's *Nanyuki Airfield, tel: 072-331 0064, www.barneysnanyuki.com.* Café serving home-baked meals, steaks, burgers, pasta and sandwiches.

Trout Tree Restaurant *Naro Moru Road, Nanyuki, tel: 062-62053/4.* Simple but delicious trout. The main restaurant is delightfully set within a Mugumo tree overlooking trout breeding ponds.

WESTERN KENYA

Coffee Shop Kitale *Main Road, next to Kitale Museum, Kitale, tel: 072-665 1361.* Set in a spacious old building with outdoor seating, this café serves fresh coffee and a varied selection of light meals.

Haandi Restaurant *Oginda Odinga Street, Kisumu, tel: 073-364 8294.* A recently opened branch of the Nairobi stalwart, this serves the best Indian food in the region with plenty of vegetarian options available.

La Belle Inn *Moi Avenue, Naivasha, tel: 050-202 1007.* Longstanding landmark in central Naivasha serving a selection of tasty and inexpensive meals and snacks on the terrace.

Nakuru Sweet Mart *Gusil Road, Nakuru.* Vegetarians will struggle to find a better lunchtime *thali* buffet anywhere in Kenya.

MOMBASA AND THE SOUTH COAST

The African Pot *Diani Beach Road, tel: 040-320 3890.* For those keen on trying the local cuisine, this dependable restaurant serves a varied selection of Swahili and upcountry dishes.

Ali Barbour's Cave *Diani Beach, tel: 071-445 6131, www.cave restaurant.com.* Soak up the beach atmosphere with good seafood and pizzas.

Aquamarine Restaurant *Mtwapa Creek, tel: 072-241 0572.* Legendary seafood restaurant known for its excellent platters. Also good for steak.

Charlie Claw's Island Restaurant *Wasini Island off Shimoni. 040-320 2331/3055, www.wasini.com.* Five-course seafood lunch: fresh, whole crab steamed in ginger, barbecue fish with Swahili sauce.

Moorings Floating Restaurant *Mtwapa Creek, tel: 041-548 5045, www.themoorings.co.ke.* Kenya's only static floating restaurant, built in 1994, this characterful stalwart is also one of the top seafood venues on the coast.

Recoda Restaurant *Nyeri Street, Mombasa Old Town, tel: 041-222 3629.* Established in 1942, this unpretentious and well-priced Swahili restaurant specialises in barbecued meat and pilau (the spicy local equivalent of risotto), but is also strong on vegetarian dishes.

Tamarind Restaurant, Dhow and Casino *Silos Road, Nyali, tel: 041-4471 747, www.tamarind.co.ke.* Very popular seafood restaurant that serves good, fresh dishes overlooking Tudor Creek and Mombasa Island.

MALINDI

Baby Marrow *Vasco da Gama Road, tel: 073-380 1238.* Open-air restaurant serving good Italian cuisine.

I Love Pizza Restaurant *Vasco da Gama Road, tel: 042-212 0672.* Inexpensive pizzas and a wide selection of vegetarian options opposite the central craft market.

Old Man and the Sea Restaurant *Vasco Da Gama Road, tel: 042-213 1106.* A small, popular seafood restaurant.

LAMU

Bush Gardens *Lamu Waterfront, tel: 042-463 3285.* Known for its seafood and kebabs, but stop in for breakfast and try the delicious mango pancakes.

Café Bastani *near Lamu House Museum, tel: 072-285 9594, email: lamuchanjo@yahoo.com.* Peaceful and leafy courtyard restaurant serving great coffee and smoothies, and a varied vegetarian-friendly selection of healthy light meals.

New Lamu Palace Hotel *Lamu waterfront, tel: 042-463 3164, www.lamuparadiseholidays.com.* Two good seafood restaurants in the hotel, the only ones in town to serve alcohol.

A–Z TRAVEL TIPS

A Summary of Practical Information

A

ACCOMMODATION

Tourist-oriented accommodation in Kenya can be divided into three distinct location-related categories, i.e. city hotels, beach resorts, and lodges and camps in national parks and reserves. Self-catering accommodation also exists in some reserves, but it is geared more towards self-drive residents than to tourists.

There is no official grading system for hotels and lodges in Kenya. It is advisable to book all accommodation in Kenya well in advance (most people do so as part of a tour or safari package), particularly in national parks and reserves, where lodges and camps tend to be very spaced out and ill-equipped to deal with passing custom.

City hotels. In Nairobi, and to a lesser extent in some small towns, accommodation geared towards tourists is dominated by multi-storey city hotels not far removed from what you'd find anywhere in the world (the likes of Hilton, InterContinental and Fairmont are all represented in Nairobi) though often with an African twist to the décor. The best of these hotels would warrant a 4–5 star rating internationally (no such rating system exists in Kenya) but they are quite pricey and have limited seasonal price variation, because their main market is business travellers and NGO workers. A welcome recent development in Nairobi has been the opening of several smaller suburban hotels, most famously perhaps Giraffe Manor, that fit somewhere between a bush camp and a boutique hotel in feel. In addition, most towns have numerous rudimentary local guesthouses, which offer little more than a bed, water and minimal security, but these are not recommended for tourists.

Beach hotels. On the coast, most people stay in one of the numerous large resorts that line beaches such as Diani, Watamu, Malindi and the coast immediately north of Mombasa. These resorts are mostly very sumptuous, albeit in a rather stereotypical way, with palm-lined beaches, large swimming pools, great seafood and villa or hotel-like accommodation. However, there are also an increasing number of smaller and more exclusive coastal properties that more closely resemble a bush camp in feel.

Lodges and camps. Most visitors to Kenya spend the bulk of their time on safari, where two types of accommodation are available. The more conventional of these, typically operated by chains such as Sopa, Sarova and Serena and aimed mainly at group tours, are large 'hotel in the bush'-style lodges whose packaged feel, high comfort levels and physical solidity are well suited to novice safari-goers and older travellers.

The alternative to these large lodges is an ever-growing choice of smaller (5- to 20-unit) bush camps that offer accommodation in en-suite walk-in tents or bandas (huts or chalets) and that blend into the surrounding bush to create a 24-hour safari experience. Many of these bush camps are surprisingly trendy in their style of décor, and genuinely luxurious, catering almost entirely to fly-in guests, for whom they provide all activities using their own experienced guides.

The choice of accommodation is most reserves is enormous – at last count, more than 50 lodges and camps in the Maasai Mara alone – and the exact location of a lodge or camp will often have a significant effect on the quality of game drives. So, in addition to consulting the listings, it is wise to talk through your priorities and options with a knowledgeable safari operator.

Self-catering. Sturdily built self-catering bandas are available in many game parks. They offer cooking facilities, which vary from a propane gas stove to a campfire, and guests are required to bring their own food and drink, and in some cases bedding. These self-catering units are popular with Kenyans during high season and public holidays, but seldom used by tourists. Bookings can be made with Kenya Wildlife Service, tel: 020-600 0800, www.kws.go.ke.

AIRPORTS

All three of Kenya's international airports, as well as seven domestic airports, are managed by the Kenya Airports Authority (KAA, www.

kenyaairports.co.ke), whose website includes a detailed overview of all amenities at the airport and scheduled departures and arrivals. Visas can be bought by those who require them upon arrival at any of the three international airports. Most package safaris will include either a transfer from the airport to your hotel, or a shuttle service provided by the hotel itself. Failing that, numerous taxis are on hand at all airports, but establish the fare before you get on board.

The most important gateway to Kenya is Nairobi's **Jomo Kenyatta International Airport** (often abbreviated to JKIA, though the official code is NBO), which lies alongside the Mombasa Road, in the suburb of Embakasi, about 10km (6 miles) southeast of the city centre. The sixth busiest airport in Africa, JKIA serves around 5 million passengers annually, and the modern facilities include 24-hour currency exchange, ATMs, a post office, internet cafés and numerous duty-free shops, as well as restaurants, coffee stops and bars. There are currently three terminals, of which Unit 1 and 2 are mainly for international flights and unit 3 is for domestic flights. A fourth terminal was under construction in early 2012.

Mombasa's **Moi International** Airport (MBA), situated on the mainland about 8km (5 miles) west of the island-bound city centre (and linked to it by a road causeway) is a less popular point of entry than JKIA, but it has good facilities and it now receives quite a number of international flights, and is particularly popular with charter beach packages. In western Kenya, **Eldoret International Airport** (EDL) receives a few cargo flights from outside the country, but it is seldom used by tourists.

With the notable exception to the national carrier Kenya Airways, whose domestic flights to/from Nairobi all use JKIA, most domestic carriers operate out of **Wilson** Airport (WIL, www.kenyaairports.co.ke), which lies about 4km (2.5 miles) south of the city centre and some 15km (9 miles) from JKIA, and handles an average of more than 300 take-offs and landings daily, almost all of them light aircraft flying to/from the Mombasa, Lamu, Masai Mara and other game reserves.

B

BUDGETING FOR YOUR TRIP

The following list will give you some idea of what to expect in Kenya; however, these prices are approximate, so add a small contingency figure to allow for inflation. The Kenya shilling and exchange rate fluctuates widely, and most tour operators and hotels quote their rates in US dollars. Otherwise, prices are given here in the local currency.

Accommodation. Rates for double room, high season: Town hotels US$150–500 (bed and breakfast); beach hotels US$200–400 (half board); package game lodges US$300–500 (full board); exclusive game lodges and tented camps US$400–1000 (full board).

Attractions. Museums/historic ruins US$6–15 per person (see www.museums.or.ke); visits to tribal villages 600–1,200Ksh; boat trips 2,000–4,000Ksh per hour.

Domestic flights. One-way flights from Nairobi–Mombasa start at US$50; Nairobi–Maasai Mara US$125 upwards; Nairobi–Lamu from around US$180. All are scheduled flights.

International flights Typically, flights from Europe start at around US$500, while those from the US or Australia are considerably more expensive

Park entrance fees. Daily entrance fees, usually valid for a 24-hour period, are US$95 per person for the Maasai Mara; US$80 for Amboseli and Lake Nakuru; US$65 for Tsavo East, Tsavo West and Meru; US$50–55 for Aberdare and Mount Kenya; US$40 for Nairobi National Park; US$20–25 for most other parks and reserves. See www.kws.org for further details.

Meals and drinks. Depending on the quality of the restaurant, main courses 400–1,500Ksh (one course), while starters and desserts are about half that; a 500ml local beer costs 150–400Ksh, a local soft drink 100–250Ksh, a glass of wine around 300–500Ksh, a bottle of wine upwards of 2,000Ksh.

C

CAMPING

Campsites are available on most national parks and reserves (see www.kws.org for details), and also at other outdoor attractions such as the Rift Valley lakes, but facilities tend to be limited at campsites, and they are seldom used by tourists (except those on budget camping safaris).

CAR HIRE

To hire a car on a self-drive basis you must be over 23 and under 70 years of age and possess a valid driver's licence from your country of residence, or an international driver's permit. The driver must have held the licence for a minimum period of two years at the time of hiring a vehicle. Many car rental companies will only rent cars with a local driver included as part of the package. Although 4-wheel-drive vehicles are not essential, they are strongly advisable for driving in game parks and reserves.

All the major international car-hire firms are represented in Kenya and numerous local firms offer competitive rates. Prices are higher than in Europe and North America. A deposit and daily collision damage insurance are compulsory. Safety rather than price should be your first consideration in choosing a car-hire firm: a breakdown in a remote area or game park is more than an inconvenience – it can pose a real danger. Confirm in writing that if the car breaks down, the car-hire company will replace it with another vehicle. Always check the oil, water, tyres, and engine; determine whether petrol or diesel is required and ensure that you have at least one good spare tyre and the essential tools. If possible, hire the car the day before setting out on the road in order to drive around town and check the condition of the vehicle.

Adventure Upgrade Safaris & Car Hire; tel: 020-228 725; www.adventureupgradesafaris.co.ke.

Avis; tel: 020-253 3610; www.avis.co.ke.

Central Rent-a-Car; tel: 020-222 2888; www.carhirekenya.com.

Elite Car Rental; tel: 020-358 1027; www.elitecarrentaltours.com.
Muthaiga Travel; tel: 020-248 9985-6; www.muthaigatravel.com.
Southern Cross Safaris; tel: 020-807 0311-6; www.southerncross
kenya.com.

CLIMATE

Since Kenya is on the equator, the climate remains pretty stable
throughout the year. Days are sunny and hot, but nights can be cool.
The weather is warm and dry from mid-December to mid-March,
and the long rains fall between late March and May. July and August
form the coldest season. September to October are the best times
to visit, as the weather is good prior to the short rains that begin in
late October through to mid-December. Coastal temperatures range
from 28°C (82°F) to 32°C (90°F) with varying degrees of humidity.

Nairobi	J	F	M	A	M	J	J	A	S	O	N	D
max °C	24	25	26	24	23	21	21	21	24	25	23	23
min °C	11	12	13	14	13	11	10	10	11	13	13	12
rainfall (mm)	65	60	90	220	175	35	18	24	30	55	155	100

Mombasa	J	F	M	A	M	J	J	A	S	O	N	D
max °C	32	32	33	31	29	28	28	28	28	30	31	32
min °C	23	24	24	24	23	21	21	20	20	22	23	25
rainfall (mm)	35	15	55	165	240	80	70	65	70	100	90	75

CLOTHING

Lightweight, cotton casual wear is fine on safari, and a hat and sun-
glasses are recommended for protection against the strong sun. Bright
colours are best avoided, as they can attract insects and make you too
conspicuous in the bush. Evenings in Nairobi are cool, and can be very
chilly in the Highlands. Warm clothing is necessary after sunset and
in early mornings. At lower altitudes, a long-sleeved shirt and long

trousers are a deterrent to mosquitoes. Trainers are the most versatile footwear – you may want to bring hiking boots if you plan to do a lot of walking in the bush, and waterproof shoes in the rainy seasons.

Nudity and topless sunbathing on beaches or in public places are forbidden.

CRIME AND SAFETY

Kenya as a whole ranks among the safest countries in Africa. In terms of common crime such as pickpocketing, confidence tricks and muggings, Nairobi – nicknamed 'nairobbery' – is the main hotspot, and it is unwise to explore the city centre without a local guide, but especially after dark. Suburban Nairobi carries fewer risks for tourists, but use taxis to get around.

Some of the beaches around Mombasa have a bad reputation for snatch theft and muggings, so avoid isolated locations. Crime levels are less significant in smaller towns, but it remains a good idea to keep out of dark backstreets at night, wherever you are, and to avoid the sleazier bars and dance dives in the coastal towns.

Most hotel rooms have a combination-lock safe, and it is strongly advised to leave all your money, important documents and other valuables here instead of lying out in the open. If your room lacks a safe, then either secure any valuables in a locked suitcase, or leave them at reception.

Kenya's shared border with troubled Somalia make it vulnerable to terrorist attacks and a spate of kidnappings attributed to Al-Shabaab (an affiliate of Al Qaeda) occurred in the far northeast of the country. As a result, the British Foreign Office currently advises against all but essential travel to coastal areas within 150km of the Somali border and within 60km of the Somali border inland from the coastal strip, and to Garissa District, an area that includes Lamu. Even if one chooses to dismiss this sort of advice as overzealous, it renders most travel insurance policies redundant within the affected zone. The situation will hopefully change for the better, so check www.fco.gov.uk and http://travel.state.gov/travel for the latest cautions.

D

DISABLED TRAVELLERS

Kenyans generally have a helpful attitude towards disabled travellers. Most of the larger hotels in town and on the coast have lifts. Traffic is a bigger problem; be careful crossing the busy streets. In the game parks, negotiating narrow stone paths at some of the lodges may be difficult in a wheelchair. Seek advice from a knowledgeable travel agent when choosing a lodge. Also, the rough, bumpy roads may cause discomfort even in the most luxurious safari vehicle.

DRIVING

Driving in many parts of Kenya is at best a challenge and at worst a nightmare. You may want to leave much of the driving, especially on unpaved dirt tracks, to experienced, well-trained tour drivers.

Driving conditions. Kenyan motorists drive on the left and overtake on the right. Most vehicles have the steering wheel on the right. Roads are narrow, so ensure you have full view of the stretch ahead before attempting to overtake. Road conditions in many places are appalling, despite ongoing upgrades to main routes. The speed limit on open roads is 80km (50 miles) per hour, but be alert to the large speed bumps (often unsignposted and almost invisible until you are right upon them) that straddle the road in almost any settlement. Drive slowly on rough roads to maintain control of your vehicle. Be prepared for unexpected manoeuvres and poor driving standards.

Dirt roads quickly turn to mud when it rains. When approaching a nasty-looking patch of mud or water, it's best to check the depth first if possible; if not, keep moving in second gear until you're clear.

Driving in the National Parks. Speeds are strictly limited to 40kph (25mph) and sometimes less, so as not to frighten the wild animals. For the same reason, avoid all loud noises and brusque movements.

Distances. Here are some approximate road distances in km (miles):

Nairobi–Eldoret	310 (190)	Mombasa–Eldoret	800 (495)
Nairobi–Kisumu	350 (215)	Mombasa–Kisumu	845 (525)
Nairobi–Malindi	615 (380)	Mombasa–Malindi	120 (75)
Nairobi–Mombasa	490 (305)	Mombasa–Marsabit	1,110 (690)
Nairobi–Nanyuki	200 (125)	Mombasa–Moyale	1,380 (855)
Nairobi–Nyeri	160 (100)	Mombasa–Nakuru	650 (405)

Traffic police. Make sure your hire car has the proper insurance and PSV (passenger service vehicle) licence stickers in case you are pulled over. For minor traffic offences, the police impose fines on the spot. You will have to appear in court and pay the fine in cash.

Breakdowns. Before setting out for long-distance driving, contact the Automobile Association of Kenya (www.aakenya.co.ke), the headquarters of which is in Nairobi. The AA will advise on the road conditions ahead, and on how to obtain help in an emergency. It can also supply you with a list of contact numbers countrywide. When travelling off the main routes, spare parts and proper tools may be scarce, and you should consider taking jerry cans of petrol and water. If you do have a breakdown in a hired vehicle, contact the rental company before you take any further action, as it may not agree to refund any repairs you pay for without their consent. If the breakdown is serious, they may send you a replacement vehicle. If not, agree a price with local mechanics before any work begins.

E

ELECTRICITY

Major towns and cities are supplied with 240 volts, 50 cycles AC. Some lodges have independent power generators, which vary in voltage. Kenyan plugs are of the three square-pin 13-amp type.

EMBASSIES AND CONSULATES

Australia: High Commission: ICIPE House, Riverside Drive, Nairobi; tel: 020-427 7100; www.kenya.embassy.gov.au.

Canada: High Commission: Limuru Road, Gigiri, Nairobi; tel: 020-366 3000 www.kenya.gc.ca.

Ireland: Consulate: Centenary House, Ring Road Westlands Lane; tel: 020-235 7242.

New Zealand: Honorary Consul, Room 2C, Mirage Plaza, Mombasa Road; tel: 020-600 1074.

South Africa: Roshanmaer Place, Lenana Road; tel: 020-282 7100.

UK: High Commission: Upper Hill Road, Nairobi; tel: 020-284 4000; http://ukinkenya.fco.gov.uk.

US: Embassy: Embassy Building, United Nations Avenue, Gigiri; tel: 020-363 6000; http://nairobi.usembassy.gov/.

EMERGENCIES

Police, Fire, Ambulance anywhere in Kenya, tel: 999 from a landline, or 112 from a mobile phone.

Emergency Plus Medical Services (24-hour ambulance and medical service owned by the Kenya Red Cross Society): Emergency hotline 0700 395395; www.eplus.co.ke.

Tourist Help Line, tel: 020-272 7844.

G

GAY AND LESBIAN TRAVELLERS

Kenya has no real gay scene and it cannot be recommended as a gay-friendly destination comparable with, say, South Africa. Male homosexual behaviour is illegal and carries a penalty of up to 14 years imprisonment. The law makes no overt mention of lesbianism, but the attitude is that homosexuality will not be tolerated. Despite this, formal gay rights are promoted through the Gay and Lesbian Coalition of Kenya (www.galck.org) and Gay Kenya (www.gaykenya.

com). In practice, travellers who happen to be gay or lesbian are unlikely to encounter any problems, provided that they are discreet about their sexuality.

GETTING TO KENYA

A high proportion of visitors to Kenya book an air ticket as part of a bespoke or package safari through an international safari operator, but it is also possible to book standalone flights. The award-winning national carrier Kenya Airways operates an extensive intra-African network, with regular flights connecting Nairobi to most of the continent's major capitals, as well as to London and several other cities in Europe, the Middle East and Asia. A user-friendly online booking service can be accessed at www.kenya-airways.com.

Other options from the UK are plentiful, since Nairobi is also serviced by most major European and African airlines, including British Airways (www.britishairways.com), Brussels Airlines (www.brusselsairlines.com), Emirates (www.emirates.com), KLM (www.klm.com), and Virgin Atlantic (www.virgin-atlantic.com). However, there are no direct flights to Kenya from the Americas or Australia, so most visitors route through London, Amsterdam or Johannesburg.

GUIDES AND TOURS

Hundreds of tour operators, both within Kenya and based outside the country, offer a range of bespoke and/or group tours to Kenya, most of which divide up into safari and beach sectors, possibly with a night or two in transit in Nairobi. Other itineraries focus solely on the safari aspect of the country, allowing one to see a fuller range of the country's natural habitats over the course of 10–14 days split between Amboseli, Maasai Mara, the Rift Valley Lakes, one of the tree hotels in the central highlands, and Laikipia and/or Samburu-Buffalo Springs. Dedicated beach packages are also available, most popularly at Diani, Watamu or Malindi, and often incorporating a short safari break to nearby Tsavo East or West.

For those who prefer to book their safari through an international operator, inclusive of flights, recommended companies include African Mecca Safaris (tel: (US) +1 866 527 4281; www.africanmeccasafaris.com), Audley Travel (tel: (UK) +44 (0)1993 838 500; www.audleytravel.com), Naturally Africa (tel: (UK) +44 (0)208 123 0301, www.naturallyafrica.co.uk) and Rainbow Tours (tel: (UK) +44 (0)20 7666 1250, www.rainbowtours.co.uk). Alternatively, you can book directly through one of several reputable Kenyan-based operators, among them Gamewatchers Safaris (tel: 077-413 6523; www.porini.com), Muthaiga Travel (tel: 020-248 9985-6; www.muthaigatravel.com) and Southern Cross Safaris (tel: 020-807 0311-6; www.southerncrosskenya.com).

H

HEALTH AND MEDICAL CARE

Medical services are better in Kenya than in most other African countries. On the coast and in Nairobi there are some first-rate hospitals with specialist physicians and surgeons, as well as some fine dentists and opticians. All visitors are strongly urged to buy full medical insurance from a reputable organisation in their home country, ideally a policy that allows for repatriation where required. Also worthwhile is the inexpensive insurance policy sold by the famous Flying Doctor Service (tel: 020-600 2299; www.amref.org), wherein a doctor will fly out from Wilson Airport to treat any casualties on the spot or fly them to a hospital in Nairobi.

Malaria. The main health hazard is malaria, which is endemic to most parts of Kenya below 1,800 metres (6,000ft), and subject to occasional outbreaks at slightly higher altitudes, such as Nairobi. Prophylactics are essential, and all prospective visitors are advised to consult a specialist travel clinic as to which pills are most appropriate for Kenya at the time you intend to travel. As an added precaution against the mosquito bites that spread the disease, wear long trousers, socks and long sleeves in the evenings, apply insect repellent to any bare skin and sleep under a mosquito net whenever possible.

Health precautions. Protection against yellow fever is an international requirement for entering Kenya, but cholera protection is not mandatory. Consult your doctor or a specialist travel clinic for advice.

Tap water is drinkable in Nairobi. Elsewhere, water should be boiled unless it has been drawn from ice-cold mountain streams. Bottled mineral water is widely available.

You can safely swim in the sea, but avoid swimming, bathing in or drinking from lakes (especially Lake Victoria), rivers or open natural reservoirs because of the risk of bilharzia, parasites, typhoid or dysentery bacilli. All swimming pools are safe and usually well cared for.

Recent figures place the rate of HIV Infection in Kenya at around 6 percent of the adult population. While this is a significant improvement on the situation in the 1990s, it is still one of the highest infection rates in the world, and the risks associated with having unprotected sex in Kenya barely need stating.

Pharmacies. There is no shortage of pharmacies (chemists) in Kenya, all of which are staffed by qualified pharmacists. Most close on Saturday afternoon, Sunday and public holidays. When closed, the name and location of the duty chemist is usually posted on the shop door. Pharmacies at the main hospitals open 24 hours a day.

Hospitals in Nairobi:

Nairobi Hospital, Argwings Kodhek Road, tel: 020-284 5000; www.nairobihospital.org.

Aga Khan Hospital, 3rd Parklands Avenue, off Limuru Road, tel: 020-366 2000; www.agakhanhospitals.org.

M.P Shah Hospital, Shivachi Road, Parklands, tel: 020-374 2763-7; www.mpshahhosp.org.

Hospitals in Mombasa:

Mombasa Hospital, off Mama Ngina Drive, tel: 041-231 2191/2; www.mombasahospital.com.

The Aga Khan Hospital Mombasa, Vanga Road off Nyerere Ave, tel: 041-221 7710-5; www.agakhanhospitals.org.

L

LANGUAGE

KiSwahili, the *lingua franca* of East Africa, was originally written in Arabic characters. When British missionaries introduced the Latin alphabet, they adopted as phonetic a transliteration as possible, so that Swahili is rather easy to pronounce. More than 40 other indigenous languages are spoken regionally in Kenya. Most people, however, speak English remarkably well, and so English, whatever accent you have, will be understood, except well off the beaten track, where you'll need Swahili. *Berlitz Swahili Phrase Book & Dictionary* should help you get by.

M

MEDIA

Kenya has four well-established English-language daily papers, *The Nation*, *The Standard* and the *Kenya Times*, and their Sunday counterparts, and the weekly *East African*. The *International Express* and the *Weekly Telegraph* provide a compilation of the week's British news and major international events. There are a wide range of English-language monthly and quarterly magazines printed in Kenya, including the magazine *Travel News & Lifestyle East Africa* and *Swara*. Many international newspapers and magazines are sold on newspaper stands and in stationers' shops in the large hotels several days later, at a price.

MONEY

Currency. Kenya's unit of currency is the Shilling (slang: Bob), divided into 100 cents (c). It is abbreviated Sh(s) and written 1/-, 2/-, etc. There are silver coins of 50c, 1/-, 5/-, 10/-, 20/- and 40/-. Banknotes come in denominations of Shs 50/-, 100/-, 200/-, 500/- and 1000/-.
Exchange control regulations. Foreign currency may be exchanged for cash only at a commercial bank, foreign exchange bureaux or an authorised hotel.

Credit cards. International credit cards are accepted in Kenya, though Visa is more widely accepted than American Express or MasterCard. Visa cards can also be used to draw local currency at ATMs in cities and towns regularly visited by tourists, but not in game reserves.

O

OPENING TIMES

Opening hours vary slightly in Nairobi, the coast and up-country towns, but in general:

Banks: 9am to 3pm Monday to Friday, 9 to 11am first and last Saturday of each month, excluding national holidays. Banks at Nairobi's international airport run a 24-hour service. There are also 24-hour ATMs that accept Visa Cards outside most banks in Kenya.

Restaurants: Breakfast is usually served 7–10am, lunch 12.30–2.30pm and dinner 7.30–9.30pm. In the larger cities some restaurants will serve until midnight and you will be able to find cafés and pizzerias that serve meals throughout the day.

Shops and museums: In larger cities, generally 8am–5 or 6pm or up to 8pm. Variable in smaller cities or rural areas.

P

POLICE

The police are generally friendly and helpful to tourists and are the most reliable source of any kind of information you may require. Tourist Police patrol the popular beaches along the coast. In an emergency, dial 999 or contact the Tourist Help Line, tel: 020-272 7844; www.kenyapolice.go.ke.

POST OFFICES

Post offices are indicated by the red and blue 'Posta' sign of the Postal Corporation of Kenya. Mail boxes are painted red. There are post offices at the main shopping centres in Nairobi and Mombasa and the international airports and major towns. Main post offices are on Haile Selassie Avenue in Nairobi and on Digo Road in Mombasa. Opening hours are usually 8.30am–1pm and 2–4.30 or 5pm Monday to Friday, and 8am–noon on Saturdays.

PUBLIC HOLIDAYS

1 January	New Year's Day
1 May	Labour Day
1 June	Madaraka (self-rule) Day
20 October	Mashujaa Day (Heroes Day)
12 December	Jamhuri (Independence) Day
25 December	Christmas Day
26 December	Boxing Day

Movable Dates
Good Friday
Easter Monday
Idd-ul-Fitr (day of feasting at the end of Ramadan)
Islamic Festivals. Muslim communities follow the Islamic calendar which varies from the Western calendar by about 11 days each year. During Ramadan, the month of fasting, most stores and cafés in Islamic districts are closed during the day, particularly in the smaller towns. Maulidi, the prophet's birthday, is a colourful celebration on the coast, especially on Lamu.

R

RELIGION

Christianity is the dominant religion of Kenya with adherents divided roughly equally among Roman Catholic, Protestant and Independent African faiths. There are also large communities of Muslims on the coast, up-country and smaller communities in the northeastern region, where people of Somali origin live. About one-third of the rural population still adheres to a variety of traditional religions. In the urban centres, mosques and temples of various eastern faiths are much in evidence.

T

TELEPHONES

When calling a Kenyan number from outside the country, the dialling code is 254 and the leading zero must be dropped from the area code. Telkom Kenya (www.telkom.co.ke) provides voice data, internet and multimedia telecommunications services. Hotel call charges are generally 50–100 percent higher than the norm. Calls within East Africa are cheaper from 8pm–8am and at weekends.

Local SIM cards can be used in most mobile phones (unless locked by the original provider), so it is worth thinking about buying one for longer stays, as international SMS (text) messaging and phone calls are very inexpensive. 'Pay As You Go' scratch cards and SIM connection kits are widely and cheaply available. The most popular mobile service is provided by Safaricom (www.safaricom.com). Other providers include the Telkom-affiliated Orange and the independent Airtel. All mobile numbers have an '07' prefix.

TIME ZONES

Kenya, like Uganda and Tanzania, is on East African Standard Time, three hours ahead of GMT (or UTC) throughout the year. There is no daylight saving and the proximity to the equator means that the difference between the length of summer and winter days is minimal.

TIPPING

Tipping is not mandatory, but it is customary in several situations. Indeed, you might sometimes feel it is impossible to get anything done without offering a 'tip'. So if you appreciate a service, tip at your discretion, but keep it moderate.

Most good hotels and restaurants include a 10 percent service on the bill, but this is an appropriate amount to add if it isn't. At railway stations and airports 50Ksh per bag is considered usual, slightly more at hotels. It is unnecessary to tip taxi drivers, as fees should be negotiated before departure. Tour drivers, however, rely on tips to make up their wages. In general around US$5–10 per passenger per day is adequate but this can be adjusted for the quality of the service given.

TOILETS

Toilets (*choo*, pronounced 'cho') are almost always indicated in English, accompanied by the standard male and female symbols. *Wanawake* (Ladies) and *Wanaume* (Gentlemen) appear in bold letters in public lavatories, which are often rather smelly by comparison to toilets in hotels and restaurants.

TOURIST INFORMATION

The **Kenya Tourist Board** (KTB, Head Office at Kenya-Re Towers, Ragati Road, Upper Hill, Nairobi, tel: 020-271 2711; www.magical kenya.com) is more concerned with marketing Kenya within the industry than with providing standard tourist information services, nevertheless, it has an informative website.

Once in the country, there are no official tourist offices or information bureaux whatsoever. Fortunately, however, most private tour companies scattered around the urban centres are fairly liberal with information and there are plenty of publications available – in the form of maps, guides of varying quality, brochures, pamphlets and *What's On* and *Going Out* magazines. Hotel receptionists are also a good source of local travel advice, whether you are seeking a good restaurant or all-night pharmacy, or want to arrange a taxi or day tour.

TRANSPORT

Most tourists are on bespoke or package safaris that include all transportation within the country, whether it be by air, or road, or a combination of the two. Domestic flights are the quickest, the easiest and (except in turbulent weather) the smoothest way of getting around, but road travel tends to be a lot cheaper, and it allows you to see far more of the countryside, which is often spectacularly scenic. Flights aside, public transport, whether by road or by rail, tends to be slow, crowded and relatively unsafe, and it doesn't service the internal road circuit of any national parks or other reserves,

Flights. A good network of domestic flights links Nairobi and other main centres to all parks and reserves, which usually have numerous airstrips allowing quick road access to all camps and lodges. Although there are several scheduled flights daily to all major reserves, the exact timing and the sequence of airstrips at which they land varies from one day to the next, depending on which camps the airline needs to drop passengers at, and collect them from. The luggage restriction on most light aircraft flights is 15kg per passenger; this includes hand luggage and is strictly enforced.

The main domestic carriers include the following:

SafariLink (www.flysafarilink.com) – extensive domestic network and user-friendly website booking daily flights connecting Nairobi Wilson to Naivasha, Tsavo West, Amboseli, Samburu, Shaba, Maasai Mara, Nanyuki, Samburu, Lewa Downs, Kiwayu and Lamu, as well as Kilimanjaro International Airport in Tanzania. **Kenya Airways** (www.kenya-airways.com) – scheduled services from JKIA to Mombasa, Malindi, Lamu and Kisumu. **Air Kenya** (www.airkenya.com) – regular flights from Wilson Airport to a similar set of destinations as SafariLink.

Buses. City buses operate in Nairobi and Mombasa but they cannot be recommended to one-off visitors because they tend to be rather crowded and slow and often frequented by petty thieves. There are supplemented minibuses known locally as matatus, which have an appalling safety record, and are to be avoided at all costs. Buses and matatus are the cheapest form of inter-city travel in Kenya, with a nationwide network wherever there are decent roads, but once again they are rough and ready, and also often rather dangerously driven.

One of the more reliable bus operators is Akamba Public Road Services, tel: 072-220 3753 or 073-333 3659 or Mombasa tel: 041-249 0269/0696; www.akambabus.com. Also recommended as above average is Coast Bus LTD; tel: 041-222 0916; www.coastbus.com.

Trains. Passenger service on the venerable railway line from Nairobi to Mombasa is an enthusiast's dream. Trains run from Nairobi to Mombasa on Mon, Wed and Fri, and the other way on Tue, Thur and Sun, leaving at 7pm and arriving between 8.30 and 9am. The old-fashioned sleepers and dining car are all a bit shabby and trains are slow, but it's still a relaxing and enjoyable way to travel. First class tickets in two-bed cabins cost US$65 per person one-way. Second-class cabins, taking four passengers, cost US$55 one-way per person. These rates include dinner and breakfast. Tickets are best reserved in advance, either directly through the ticket office at Nairobi or Mombasa station, or through Kenya Train Travel (www.kenyatraintravel.com), a specialist operator that takes PayPal and credit cards

Taxis There are a number of reputable taxi operators in Nairobi and Mombasa. They do not have meters, so establish the fare before getting in. Always check with the hotel reception about the approximate charge for a journey before boarding the vehicle. Private taxis come under no particular control and the vehicles may not be properly insured. Charges for waiting time and extra passengers are negotiable.

One of Kenya's top safari companies since the early 1960s, Southern Cross (www.southerncrosskenya.com) has a large and varied fleet of 4x4s and other vehicles, and it will tailor safaris and tours to suit all interest groups, from birdwatchers and honeymooners to family groups and corporate travellers.

V

VISA AND ENTRY REQUIREMENTS

All visitors must be in possession of a valid passport with an expiry date at least six months after the end of their intended stay in Kenya.

Visas are required by everyone except citizens of some Common-wealth countries and certain countries with which Kenya has recip-rocal waiver arrangements.

Citizens of the UK, Ireland, US, Australia, Canada, New Zealand and most European countries require visas. South Africans don't require a visa for a stay of less than 30 days, but do require one for a longer stay.

Fortunately, visas can now be obtained upon arrival at any in-ternational airport and most overland borders to Kenya. This is a quick and straightforward procedure. Single entry visas cost US$50, multiple-entry US$100 and transit US$20.

Those who prefer to apply for a visa in advance should obtain an application form from the nearest Kenyan Embassy or High Com-mission, and allow at least a week for processing.

Since these arrangements may change, it is essential to double-check on visa requirements with airlines, tour operators or Kenyan High Commissions or consulates abroad well ahead of the trip.

W

WEBSITES AND INTERNET ACCESS

There are many internet cafés in Kenya's major cities and towns. Wi-Fi and/or standard internet facilities are also available in most urban hotels, and even in some safari camps and lodges, though often at inflated rates. It is also possible to pick up internet on a mobile phone with a local SIM card. However, connections tend to be erratic and slow in remote bush locations, so it is probably wise to tell rela-tives and friends that you will be offline for the duration of any safari.

www.katokenya.org Kenya Association of Tour Operators
www.kws.org Kenya Wildlife Service
www.laikipia.org Laikipia Wildlife Forum
www.magicalkenya.com Kenya Tourist Board
www.mck.or.ke Mountain Club of Kenya
www.museums.or.ke National Museums of Kenya

Recommended Hotels

Price categories are for a double room. These are based on advertised rack rates, which are normally quoted in US Dollars, and are often higher than rates charged to operators, or available for direct online bookings. Almost invariably, rates at game lodges and tented camps in national parks and private reserves include all meals, and some more exclusive properties also include activities and/or drinks. The standard package at most beach hotel and resorts is dinner, bed and breakfast, though some 'club' style resorts also include lunch and drinks. Most city hotels are bed and breakfast only, though again there are a few full-board and all-inclusive exceptions. If in doubt check the meal plan when you make a booking and again upon arrival.

$$$$	over US$500
$$$	US$300–500
$$	US$150–300
$	less than US$150

NAIROBI

Fairmont Norfolk Hotel $$$$ *Harry Thuku Road, City Centre, tel: 020-226 5555, www.fairmont.com.* Nairobi's oldest hotel is set in lovely gardens, with an aviary, swimming pool, health club, beauty salon, gourmet restaurant and the Lord Delamere Terrace bar and restaurant. Have tea on the terrace or a gin and tonic in the bar and you'll catch a whiff of past colonial decades.

Fairview Hotel $$ *Bishops Road, tel: 020-271 1321, www.fairview kenya.com.* Set in 2ha (5 acres) of beautiful gardens about 2km (1 mile) from the city centre and in the tradition of a country hotel. Amenities include pool and four restaurants. Family owned.

Giraffe Manor $$$$ *Koitobos Road, Langata, tel: 020-231 6756, www. giraffemanor.com.* This prestigious small hotel at the AFEW Giraffe Centre is set in a luxurious period-furnished 1930s manor surrounded by grassy lawns and fever tree forest. The rates include superb three-course meals, with giraffes frequently poking their heads through the windows during breakfast and lunch.

Hogmead $$$$ *Mukoma Road, Langata, tel: 020-211 5453, www. hogmead.com.* Nestled within large green gardens bordering the Giraffe Centre, this stylish owner-managed lodge has six spacious and individually decorated rooms whose immense bathrooms have tub and shower. The relaxed management style and excellent food make it the perfect suburban retreat between safaris.

House of Waine $$$ *Cnr Masai Lane and Bogani Rd, Karen, tel: 020 2601455/7, www.houseofwaine.com.* One of Nairobi's most perennially popular boutique hotels, this 1970s mansion lies in large gardens in the leafy suburb of Karen, just 2km (1.2 mile) from the Karen Blixen Museum. The 11 rooms are all individually decorated reflecting various ethnic themes, but come with all modern amenities. The highly rated kitchen can offer a spread of Kenyan dishes by request.

Nairobi Serena Hotel $$$ *Cnr Nyerere Road and Kenyatta Avenue, tel: 020 2822000, www.serenahotels.com.* Combining international five-star standards with Pan-African decor, this modern hotel set in tropical gardens on the periphery of the city centre has an excellent swimming pool, gym, sauna and steam bath. There are four restaurants, including the very upmarket Mandhari and Ethiopian-styled Aksum Bar. A member of Leading Hotels of the World.

Tribe Hotel $$$ *Limuru Road, tel: 020-720 0000, www.tribe-hotel. com.* Included in the Conde Nast Traveller Hot List for 2010, this funky boutique hotel combines innovative décor with modern facilities including an excellent spa and business centre. It also offers direct foot access to the Village Market, a vast mall with myriad shops and restaurants.

Wildebeest Camp $ *Kibera Road, off Ngong Road, tel: 020-210 3505, www.wildebeestcamp.com.* This relaxed and sociable owner-managed camp has good-value standing tents with en-suite showers, as well as dormitory beds and a campsite. Facilities include inexpensive meals, internet access and an in-house safari operator.

SAMBURU AND SHABA NATIONAL RESERVES

Samburu Game Lodge $$$ *North bank of the Ewaso Ngiro River, tel: 064-30781, www.wildernesslodges.co.ke.* International facilities with comfortable accommodation in cottages, rooms and suites. Entertainment areas overlook the Ewaso Nyiro River. The Crocodile Bar allows close viewing of crocodiles and other wildlife on the opposite bank.

Samburu Sopa Lodge $$$ *Set on a hillside about 15km (9 miles) north of the river, tel: 020-375 0235, www.sopalodges.com.* This smart but relatively affordable lodge overlooks a small waterhole that attracts plenty of wildlife. The 30 rooms, laid out in an arc intended to resemble buffalo horns, are spacious and colourfully decorated, with two queen-sized beds each.

Sarova Shaba Lodge $$$ *South bank of the Ewaso Nyiro River, tel: 020-231 5139, www.sarovahotels.com.* Boasting a wonderfully isolated riverfront location in lush grounds bisected by several spring-fed streams, this 80-room lodge has an unusually wild feel for its size, with in-house game viewing ranging from hippos and crocs along the river to plentiful birds and monkeys in the trees.

THE CENTRAL HIGHLANDS

The Ark $$$$ *Eastern slopes of the Aberdares, tel: 020-210 1333, www.thearkkenya.com.* Recently reopened under new management, this upmarket tree hotel, named for its boat-like shape, is entered along a gangplank above the trees. Sightings of elephant, rhino, waterbuck, leopard, buffalo and genet are likely.

Il Ngwesi Lodge $$$$. *North of Lewa Wildlife Conservancy, tel: 020-203 3122, www.ilngwesi.com.* An award-winning community eco-lodge, built with local materials. The Maasai hosts look after the lodge and visitors' needs. The six bandas, lounge and swimming pool afford stunning views of Kenya's Northern Frontier District.

Lewa House $$$$ *Lewa Wildlife Conservancy, tel: 064-31405, www.lewa.org.* This small lodge combines luxurious accommodation and a homely atmosphere with superb game drives, guided walks and – a speciality – horseback safaris in an area densely populated by rhinos, elephants, big cats and the localised Grevy's zebra.

Mount Kenya Safari Club $$$$ *8km (5 miles) southeast of Nanyuki, tel: 020-226 5555, www.fairmont.com.* Established as a retreat for the international jet set by the late Hollywood star William Holden in 1959, this remains a highly luxurious hotel, set in vast landscaped gardens that incorporate the Mount Kenya Wildlife Conservancy. Superb food. Heated swimming pool, golf course, tennis, horseback riding, croquet lawn, aviary.

Naro Moru River Lodge $–$$ *Naro Moru, tel: 072-408 2754, www. naromoruriverlodge.com.* This affordable lodge, set in pretty wooded grounds bounded by the Naro Moru River, is a good place to organise on-the-ground ascents of Mount Kenya.

Porini Rhino Camp $$$$ *Ol Pejeta Ranch, tel: 077-413 6523, www. porini.com.* This isolated tented camp has near-exclusive use of the western part of Ol Pejeta Ranch, home to dense numbers of cheetah, lion, white rhino, black rhino and elephant. It is a classic bush camp, comprising six comfortable en-suite tents strung along a seasonal watercourse, and the standard of service and guiding is excellent.

Serena Mountain Lodge $$$$ *Mount Kenya, about 35km (20 miles) from Karatina, tel: 020-284 2000, www.serenahotels.com.* Tree hotel in the heart of the rainforest. Most rooms have balconies overlooking the waterhole, where buffalo, antelope, elephant, giant forest hog and, sometimes lion and leopard visit. Sykes monkeys clamber along the roof and ledges (and into your room if given the chance). At 2,195m (7,200ft) nights are chilly (hot-water bottles provided), so bring an extra layer such as a fleece. Jungle walks with excellent guides and relaxing beauty treatments available.

Serena Sweetwaters Tented Camp $$$–$$$$ *Ol Pejeta Ranch, tel: 020-284 2000, www.serenahotels.com.* Accommodation is in luxury tents that ring one side of the waterhole, allowing you to be out in the open air with the animals, but protected by an electric fence. There are 40 twin tents, all en-suite with hot water, electricity and flushing toilets. Other attractions include a swimming pool, camel rides, a chimp sanctuary, night game drives and nature walks.

Solio Camp $$$$ *Solio Ranch, tel: 020-502 0888, www.tamimiea. com.* This luxurious new lodge comprises six individually-decorated glass-fronted suites built on a scale such that the bathrooms – with tub and shower – are as large as the average hotel room. Game drives come with your best chance of close-up black rhino sightings in Kenya, white rhino are even more common, and lion and cheetah are also likely to be seen, along with plentiful plains grazers.

Treetops $$–$$$ *Eastern slopes of the Aberdares, tel: 020-445 2095-9, www.aberdaresafarihotels.com.* The original tree hotel, and model for the more modern Serena Mountain Lodge and The Ark, Treetops no longer offers game viewing to compare with its younger rivals, but it has plenty of character and is under renovation and expansion. Elephant and buffalo are seen most days.

THE GREAT RIFT VALLEY

Lake Bogoria Spa Resort $–$$ *Lake Bogoria National Reserve, tel: 020-224 9055, www.lakebogoria-hotel.com.* The only tourist-class accommodation in the vicinity of Lake Bogoria is a bit character-less but comfortable enough at the asking price. There's a naturally heated Olympic-sized pool, and guided bird walks in the gardens.

Lake Naivasha Sopa Resort $$$ *South Lake Road, Lake Naivasha, tel: 020-375 0235, www.sopalodges.com.* Set in expansive lakeshore grounds studded with beautiful stands of yellow fever trees, this lodge has 85 suite-like rooms with private balconies or solariums. Nature walks in the bird-rich gardens, and boats on to the lake.

Mbweha Camp $$$ *Outside Lake Nakuru NP, 20 minutes drive from Nderit Gate, tel: 020-445 0035-6, www.atua-enkop.com.* Set in the Con-greve Conservancy, which shares its western border with Lake Na-kuru National Park, this has far more of a 'bush' feel than any lodge in the national park, comprising just 10 spacious solar-powered stone-and-thatch chalets surrounded by indigenous candelabra and yellow-barked acacia trees.

Sanctuary Farm $$ *South Lake Road, Lake Naivasha, tel: 072-276 1940, www.sanctuaryfarmkenya.com.* Likeable and affordable family-run lodge is set on a 500-acre working farm inhabited by large numbers of giraffe, zebra and antelope and linked to Crescent Island by a causeway. Horse riding, walking and boating are all on offer.

Samatian Island Lodge $$$$ *Lake Baringo, tel: 072-723 2445, www. samatianislandlodge.com.* This exclusive island camp consists of seven spectacular open-fronted thatched lake-facing chalets that feel like an extension of the surrounding jungle. It's a great place to chill out, with a lovely infinity pool and plenty of small wildlife rustling around, while more active visitors can take a canoe out on the lake.

Sarova Lion Hill Lodge $$$ *Lake Nakuru National Park, tel: 020-231 5139, www.sarovahotels.com.* Overlooking the eastern lakeshore, this is the pick of the two lodges set within Lake Nakuru National Park, with a great location and amenities such as a swimming pool, spa and excellent buffet restaurant.

WESTERN KENYA

Barnley's Guest House $ *8km (5 miles) from Saiwa Swamp, tel: 073-713 3170, www.sirikwasafaris.com.* This family-run lodge, set in lovely green gardens alive with birds and monkeys, is a popular base for day trips to Saiwa Swamp and Mount Elgon national parks.

Kiboko Bay Resort $$ *5km south of central Kisumu, tel: 057-202 5510, www.kibokobay.com.* The genuine lakeshore resort in Kisumu offers a dozen comfortable ensuite standing tents, a great restaurant (specialising in Indian dishes and fresh fish), a swimming pool, and regular visits by hippos at night.

Mfangano Island Camp $$$$ *Lake Victoria, tel: 020-273 4000, www. governorscamp.com.* Small exclusive camp, accessible by light aircraft and speedboat, set in natural tropical gardens in a secluded island bay. Just six rooms, which are in traditional Luo tribal style with mud walls and thatched roofs.

Rondo Retreat $$ *Kakamega Forest, tel: 056-30268, www.rondoretreat.com.* This tranquil Christian-run retreat has three rooms using shared bathrooms in the main building, as well as 15 ensuite cottages, and a reputation for hearty food (but no alcohol is served), and the surrounding area offers wonderful birdwatching.

MAASAI MARA NATIONAL RESERVE

Bateleur Camp $$$$ *Mara Triangle, tel: 020-374 5238, www.and beyondafrica.com.* Set in a private conservancy at the forested base of the Oloololo Escarpment, this stylish luxury tented camp has a stunning location, fine food, a good selection of house wines (included in the room rates), and expert guiding on game drives in the remote Mara Triangle.

Governors' Camps $$$$ *Central Mara, tel: 020-2734000, www. governorscamp.com.* Four superb old-style tented camps. All tents have en-suite bathrooms with constant hot and cold running water and flushing toilets. There is a bar tent and a dining tent with views over the plains; for more intimacy, try the Little Governors' Camp.

Porini Lion Camp $$$ *Olare Orok Conservancy, tel: 077-413 6523, www.porini.com.* A good choice for those looking for an eco-safari, this is one of a handful of small camps scattered around the 300 sq km (115 sq mile) Olare Orok Conservancy, comprising ten en-suite tents along the wooded Ntiakatiak River and operating on a similar community-oriented formula to Porini Mara.

Porini Mara Camp $$$$ *Ol Kinyei Conservancy, tel: 077-413 6523, www.porini.com.* Accommodating up to 12 guests, this exclusive tented bush camp has sole traversing rights over the 150 sq km (58 sq mile) Ol Kinyei Conservancy, a Maasai concession that supports a similar cross section of habitats and wildlife to the Mara, including one of Kenya's largest lion prides. The ultimate eco-safari destination, it is perhaps the last place in the greater Mara where you'll have most of your sightings to yourself.

Rekero Camp $$$$ *Central Mara, tel: 020-232 4904, www.asilia africa.com.* Comprising nine standing tents, carved in lush riverine woodland, with balconies facing a rocky stretch of the Talek River, this luxurious camp is well positioned both for general game viewing and for the wildebeest crossings. Food and service are excellent.

Riverside Camp $–$$ *Near Talek Gate, tel: 072-021 8319, www.river sidecampmara.com.* This Maasai-owned community camp is about the most inexpensive camp in the greater Mara, with a stunning location bordering the reserve's central sector. Simple but comfortable bandas are available, and camping is permitted.

THE SOUTHEAST

AMBOSELI NATIONAL PARK

Amboseli Porini Camp $$$$ *Selenkay Conservation Area, tel: 077-413 6523, www.porini.com.* Great for those wanting a proper eco-safari, this award-winning camp consists of nine comfortable en-suite standing tents set in a vast community reserve to which it has exclusive traversing rates.

Amboseli Serena Lodge $$$ *Enking Narok Swamp, tel: 020-284 2000, www.serenahotels.com.* Solid and well-run lodge with 96 comfortable rooms grouped like a Maasai village. The novel dining room has a stream running through it.

Satao Elerai Camp $$$$ *Elerai Conservancy, tel: 020-243 4600-3, www.sataoelerai.com.* Luxurious and architecturally innovative, this remote camp comprising nine en-suite standing tents and five large thatch suites runs along a rocky ridge offering expansive views over the Amboseli Plains towards Kilimanjaro.

Tortilis Camp $$$$ *Kitirua Conservancy, tel: 020-600 3090-1, www. chelipeacock.com.* Award-winning eco-tourism camp with 17 spacious tents, excellent food, swimming pool, game drives, guided nature walks and great views of Kilimanjaro.

TSAVO WEST NATIONAL PARK AND ENVIRONS

Finch Hatton's $$$$ *Outside the northwest park boundary, tel: 020-357 7500, www.finchhattons.com.* This camp, named after the early 20th-century hunter-adventurer Denys Finch Hatton, is the height of luxury, with decor featuring antiques, chandeliers and crystal glasses. There is also a swimming pool and top-notch cuisine.

Kilaguni Serena Safari $$$ *30km from Mtito Andei Gate, tel: 020-284 2000, www.serenahotels.com.* The first lodge built in a Kenyan National Park, Kilaguni (meaning 'young rhino') overlooks a busy waterhole with the Chyulu hills and (in clear weather) Kilimanjaro as a backdrop.

Tsavo Inn $ *Mtito Andei, tel: 072-037 9939.* This venerable hotel doesn't compare to the lodges within the park for quality, but – situated less than five minutes' drive from the entrance gate – it makes for a great budget base for game drives. There's a swimming pool and adequate restaurant.

Ziwani Voyager Camp $$$ *Ziwani Gate, tel: 020-444 6651, www.heritage-eastafrica.com.* Comprising 25 en-suite standing tents scattered in a fever tree forest fringing the Sante River, this child-friendly safari camp has a classic bush atmosphere.

TSAVO EAST NATIONAL PARK AND ENVIRONS

Galdessa Camp $$$$ *South bank of Galana River, tel: 040-320 2217, www.galdessa.com.* Gorgeous camp on the banks of the Galana River overlooking the Yatta Plateau.

Satao Tented Camp $$-$$$$ *Southeast of Aruba Dam, tel: 020-243 4600-3, www.sataocamp.com.* Overlooking a waterhole that frequently attracts several hundred elephants per day (along with plenty of other wildlife), this low-key and eco-friendly tented camp offers lies in the best part of the park for wildlife viewing and birding.

Voi Safari Lodge $$ *Near Voi entrance gate, tel: 020-224 4173, www.safari-hotels.com.* The clifftop position overlooking a productive waterhole is hard to beat, but unfortunately the mediocre rooms and food, while adequate at the price, don't live up to the location.

MOMBASA AND THE COAST

Diani Reef Beach Resort & Spa $$–$$$ *Diani Beach, tel: 040-320 2723, www.dianireef.com.* This bright modern resort is one of the largest and smartest on Diani. It is set on a lovely palm-fringed stretch of beach, and amenities include ten bars and restaurants, two freeform swimming pools, a gym and spa, and a good selection of watersports and excursions.

Msambweni Beach House $$$$ *Msambweni Village, tel: 020-357 7093, www.msambweni-beach-house.com.* A contender for the country's most sumptuous beach destination, this sprawling clifftop beach house has only six suites and villas, all vastly spacious with a traditional Swahili feel – plenty of arches and alcoves, whitewashed exteriors, and makuti thatch roofs. It has the largest infinity pool in Kenya, secluded baobab-studded beach, and superb food.

Pinewood Beach Resort & Spa $$$ *Galu Beach, tel: 020-208 0981-3, www.pinewood-village.com.* Set on one of the most secluded and attractive beaches on Diani, this smallish family-owned resort also has a very good dive centre, a swimming pool, spa, and plenty of birds and monkeys in the green gardens.

Sentrim Castle Royal Hotel $ *Moi Avenue, Mombasa, tel: 073-385 2083, www.castlemsa.com.* The pick of a limited selection of hotels in central Mombasa, this four-storey colonial relict has a pleasant shaded balcony where you can relax over a chilled drink or a light meal.

WATAMU

Hemingways $$$–$$$$ *Tel: 042-233 2052, www.hemingways.co.ke.* A member of the Small Luxury Hotels of the World, Hemingways has 76 airy rooms and suites, all with air-conditioning, fan and mini-bar. Catering strongly to the British market, it offers excellent service and food, with seafood being the speciality. It is renowned for its deep sea fishing, snorkelling and diving opportunities, but it's also a great place to laze around the swimming pool or on the idyllic beach.

Turtle Bay Beach Club $$ *tel: 042-233 2003, www.turtlebay.co.ke.* This family-oriented all-inclusive 145-room resort lies in large grounds with a vast freeform swimming pool, access to an excellent beach, three bars, three restaurants, three bars and a reputable dive and watersports centre. Very good value.

MALINDI

Driftwood Beach Club $$ *Silversands beach, 3km south of the town, tel: 042-212 0155, www.driftwoodclub.com.* Comprising 29 thatched cottages and villas scattered in large tropical gardens running down to a pretty beach, this good value resort is popular with Kenya residents and well suited to families.

LAMU

New Lamu Palace Hotel $$ *Lamu waterfront, south of the fort, tel: 042-463 3164, www.lamuparadiseholidays.com.* The top hostelry in Lamu Town, and a well-known waterfront landmark, this is one of the few restaurants in town to serve alcohol. The 22 en-suite rooms, though rather small, are all air-conditioned, and the four-poster king-size beds have walk-in netting.

Palm Beach House $ *About 200m inland of Lamu Museum, near Utukini Mosque, tel: 072-561 7996, www.lamuvilla.com.* Formerly known as Baytulkher, this traditional four-storey house ranks among the most characterful places to stay in the old town, containing just four large guest rooms, each individually decorated rooms in traditional Swahili style. Good value.

Peponi Hotel $$$ *Shela Beach, 3km from Lamu Town, tel: 020-802 3655, www.peponi-lamu.com.* Owned and managed by the same family since it opened in 1967, this delightful 24-room hotel has a wonderful waterfront location at Shela, Swahili-style architecture, and an attractive freeform swimming pool set under baobab trees and overlooking the ocean. Plenty of activities are offered, and the seafood and Swahili style curries are excellent.

Red Pepper House $$$$ *5 minutes north of town by motorised dhow, tel: 020-251 3147, www.theredpepperhouse.com.* Set in sprawling green grounds on a private beach, this sumptuous honeymoon-friendly resort consists of five ultra-spacious private villas that combine easy-on-the-eye Swahili architecture with the open-air feel of the country's finest bush lodges. There's a swimming pool, a dhow for private excursions, some of the best food on the coast, and a good selection of house wines.

INDEX

Berlitz pocket guide

Kenya

Fourth Edition 2012

Written by Donna Dailey
Updated by Philip Briggs
Edited by Rebecca Lovell
Picture Researcher: Lucy Johnston
Series Editor: Tom Stainer
Production: Tynan Dean, Linton Donaldson
and Rebeka Ellam

Printed in China by CTPS

Berlitz Trademark Reg. U.S. Patent Office
and other countries. Marca Registrada.
Used under licence from the Berlitz
Investment Corporation

Photography credits: AA World Travel Library
50; Alex Edwards 3TC, 17; Corbis 18, 20, 23;
Fotolia 54; 63; Ariadne Van Zandbergen/APA
2TL, 2TR, 2CR, 3TL, 3ML, 3MR, 3BL, 3BR, 4ML,
4MR, 4RT, 4TL, 4TL, 4/5 (all pics), 8, 11, 12,
15, 26, 29, 31, 32, 33, 34, 35, 37, 39, 40, 42, 43,
45, 46, 49, 53, 55, 59, 60/61, 65, 66, 69, 70, 73,
75, 76, 77, 78, 79, 81, 82, 85, 86, 89, 90, 92, 94,
97, 98, 100, 101, 103, 104; Glyn Genin 2BL
iStockphoto 1, 57

Cover picture: Corbis

Every effort has been made to provide
accurate information in this publication,
but changes are inevitable. The publisher
cannot be responsible for any resulting
loss, inconvenience or injury.

Contact us

At Berlitz we strive to keep our guides as
accurate and up to date as possible, but if you
find anything that has changed, or if you have
any suggestions on ways to improve this guide,
then we would be delighted to hear from you.

Berlitz Publishing, PO Box 7910,
London SE1 1WE, England.
email: berlitz@apaguide.co.uk
www.berlitzpublishing.com